MEETING COMMON CORE TECHNOLOGY STANDARDS

Strategies for Grades K-2

D1605041

Valerie Morrison | Stephanie Novak | Tim Vanderwerff

International Society for Technology in Education
EUGENE, OREGON • ARLINGTON, VA

Meeting Common Core Technology Standards
Strategies for Grades K-2
Valerie Morrison, Stephanie Novak, and Tim Vanderwerff

© 2016 International Society for Technology in Education

Editor: Paul Wurster
Associate Editor: Emily Reed
Production Manager: Christine Longmuir
Copy Editors: Jennifer Weaver-Neist, Kristin Landon
Cover Design: Brianne Beigh
Book Design and Production: Jeff Puda

Library of Congress Cataloging-in-Publication Data
Names: Morrison, Valerie, author. | Novak, Stephanie (Stephanie M.), author. | Vanderwerff, Tim, author.
Title: Meeting Common Core Technology Standards: Strategies for Grades K-2 / Valerie Morrison, Stephanie Novak, and Tim Vanderwerff.
Description: First edition. | Eugene, Oregon : International Society for Technology in Education, 2016. | Includes bibliographical references and index.
Identifiers: LCCN 2015035738| ISBN 9781564843685 (paperback) | ISBN 9781564845078 (ebook)
Subjects: LCSH: Education, Elementary–United States–Computer assisted instruction. | Education, Elementary–Curricula–United States. | Educational technology–United States. | Common Core State Standards (Education) | BISAC: EDUCATION / Teaching Methods & Materials / General. | EDUCATION / Computers & Technology.
Classification: LCC LB1028.5 .M6376 2016 | DDC 372.133/4–dc23 LC record available at http://lccn.loc.gov/2015035738

First Edition
ISBN: 978-1-56484-368-5 (paperback)
Ebook version available

Printed in the United States of America

ISTE® is a registered trademark of the International Society for Technology in Education.

About ISTE

The International Society for Technology in Education (ISTE) is the premier non-profit organization serving educators and education leaders committed to empowering connected learners in a connected world. ISTE serves more than 100,000 education stakeholders throughout the world.

ISTE's innovative offerings include the ISTE Conference & Expo, one of the biggest, most comprehensive ed tech events in the world—as well as the widely adopted ISTE Standards for learning, teaching and leading in the digital age and a robust suite of professional learning resources, including webinars, online courses, consulting services for schools and districts, books, and peer-reviewed journals and publications. Visit iste.org to learn more.

Contents

About the Authors

 **VALERIE MORRISON** graduated with an elementary education degree from Northern Illinois University (NIU) and began her career as a classroom teacher. She became interested in teaching with technology early on and was a computer teacher for two years at a K–8 private school. Morrison then switched to the public school system, where she obtained a master's degree in instructional technology with an emphasis in media literacy from NIU. She gained 14 years of experience as a technology director/technology integration specialist and technology coach. Morrison worked closely with teachers and students to plan and differentiate lessons and projects that integrate technology. She taught technology workshops and classes for teachers and oversaw the technology program at her school. (She loves working with kids, teachers, and technology!) Like her coauthor Tim Vanderwerff, Morrison regularly served on her district's technology committee, and was involved with integrating current state and district standards with the latest educational technologies. She presented at various conferences, including a presentation in Springfield, Illinois, to state legislators, where she and coauthor Stephanie Novak briefed legislators on how schools use technology. Morrison has recently switched career paths and is now teaching education classes at the college level; she enjoys using technology to teach the next generation of teachers. She also has time to write now, which allows her to further educate the current generation of teachers.

 **STEPHANIE NOVAK** knew from a very young age that teaching and working with kids was the right career path for her. She graduated from Northern Illinois University with a master's degree in reading and earned a reading specialist certificate from National Louis University. Novak started teaching at the middle school level but eventually settled in the elementary school system. As a classroom teacher for 27 years and an extended-learning teacher and coach for the past seven years, she has always felt learning should be fun and meaningful. Novak was on her school district's technology committee for many years and regularly tried new technology in her classroom. As an instructional coach, she encouraged teachers to help students grow in their learning at a pace that allows for the most intellectual and personal growth. For the past two years, Novak guided Grade 1–5 teachers through the Common Core State Standards, teaching them how to blend these standards with rigorous curriculum and prepare students for the digital age. After many years in

education, Novak recently retired. She now looks forward to applying her years of experience in a consulting capacity for administrators, teachers, and students. She also plans to continue to publish stories that describe her successful experiences in the field of education.

 **TIM VANDERWERFF** has an extensive background in teaching and technology that began in the '70s. Although writing this book was a new experience, trying out new experiences in education are second nature to him. After graduating from Illinois State University and then earning a master's in educational administration from Northern Illinois University, Vanderwerff saw many federal and state initiatives come and go in his 33 years of teaching. Starting as a classroom teacher in Grades 2–5, he was on his school district's technology committee for many years and regularly tried new technology in his class during that time. Vanderwerff eventually moved to the library media center at his elementary school in 1987. He was the librarian and the technology teacher, and he provided tech support for the building for many years. In 2010, he was asked to be a teaching coach, which involved sitting in on grade-level team meetings, finding resources for the new Common Core State Standards, supporting individual teachers and teams in the classroom (both with technology and with the newest educational strategies), and advising new teachers. Vanderwerff is recently retired, allowing him to devote more time to writing about the field in which he is so passionate.

DEDICATIONS

For my three daughters–Allana, LeeAnn, and Annaleese–who motivate me to continue to want to inspire educators for the sake of children.
   –Valerie Morrison

To Bill; all my family; my confidant, Kim; and my District 96 friends.
   –Stephanie Novak

To my family: Kim, Eric, Michael and Kristina.
   –Tim Vanderwerff

Acknowledgments

We are grateful for the contributions of our friends, teammates, colleagues, and assistants with whom we worked throughout the years and who helped us come up with ideas for the four books in this series. Working with so many talented people, we appreciate the collaboration and teamwork that allowed us to learn a great deal about coaching and technology. We would especially like to thank Kathy Angel and Nicci Nielsen for their contributions to the "Practical Ideas" chapters in this book (K–2).

We would also like to thank our families for all of their amazing support during the writing of this series. During the many times we spent meeting, editing, and struggling to write, their unwavering support was truly appreciated.

Also, we would like to thank the editors and staff at ISTE for their insight, guidance, and patience. Their ongoing support has been much appreciated as we've gotten familiar with the process of publishing.

Introduction

Have you ever found yourself sitting in a meeting wondering, "How am I ever going to change all my lessons to fit the new Common Core State Standards?" At that moment, you also realize your district wants you to integrate the latest digital-age technology, and that has you asking yourself, "Where will I get this technology? Will it be provided for me, or am I responsible for purchasing and providing the technology?"

All of this might seem overwhelming—what is a teacher to do? First, you might turn to your teammates and colleagues for help and support. Perhaps your district provides current technology development for staff on a regular basis and has instructional coaches to help teachers chart this new territory, planning new lessons, bringing in resources, and infusing technology. In reality, most districts don't have all of this support. Yet teachers are especially in need of technology when considering their clientele: students.

Until recently, every state was doing their own thing when it came to standards. The Common Core State Standards (CCSS) is a U.S. education initiative seeking to bring diverse state curricula into alignment with each other by following the principles of standards-based education reform. The CCSS is sponsored by the National Governors Association Center for Best Practices (NGA Center) and the Council of Chief

State School Officers (CCSSO), and a vast majority of the 50 U.S. states are members of the initiative. So, if you are in a Common Core state, there are big changes happening. Even if you're in a state that's not adopting Common Core, there is a high likelihood your curriculum will soon look very similar to the CCSS initiative.

We, as coaches, have an important role in helping you, the teachers, and your students during this transition. Our hope is that you are in a district that provides high-quality professional learning experiences regularly to help teachers understand the shift from existing state standards to the CCSS. Professional development, along with this book and its resources, will help you identify the changes you will need to make to guide your instruction using CCSS with technology and support you in transferring new knowledge and skills to the classroom. It is a large task, but focusing on specific goals for student learning utilizing the CCSS with technology will have a positive effect on student achievement. And this will improve your teaching.

CCSS were designed to prepare K–12 students for college and career success in the areas of English language arts, math, science, and social studies. CCSS defines the knowledge and skills students should have in their K–12 education, with an emphasis on learning goals as well as end-of-year expectations.

Most states have had English language arts and math standards in place for a few years. However, these standards vary, not only in coverage but also in levels of rigor. CCSS is very explicit about what is expected of students at each grade level. Students, parents, teachers, and school administrators can now work together toward common goals. CCSS will be consistent from school to school among states choosing to adopt the standards. If students or teachers transfer to different schools, they will all be assured that learning expectations will be the same. Any student, no matter where they live within a Common Core state, can be assured that they will be able to graduate from high school, get ready for college, and have a successful career.

The standards first launched in June 2009. State leaders from the CCSSO and NGA developed them together with parents, teachers, school administrators, and experts from across the country. Both national and international research and evidence informed development of the standards. After public comment, organizers released the final version of the CCSS in June 2010.

The CCSS were written in a clear, understandable, and consistent manner to align with college and work expectations. These standards contain rigorous content, as well as an application of knowledge through higher-order skills. CCSS are evidence based, and they build on the strengths and lessons of current state standards.

Writers of CCSS also gathered information and advice from top-performing countries to ensure that U.S. students are prepared to succeed in a global economy and society. Here is a helpful link from the Common Core State Standards Initiative's **"About the Standards"** page: **(http://tinyurl.com/26f7amp)**.

Transition to the Common Core will be a challenging task for your students as well as for you. With the implementation of these new standards, students will be expected to become self-directed and critical readers, writers, and thinkers. At the same time, you will need to make adjustments. In fact, you will need to shift your entire instructional practice.

Shifting your instructional practice will require a great deal of work and commitment, but this will all be well worth the effort for both you and your students. By breaking things down into small steps, the transition will seem less overwhelming.

This book is the first of a collection of four books designed to help teachers connect technology to the Common Core in their classrooms. We learned how to do this by teaching together, and we have more than 85 years of combined teaching experience. As teammates, we worked with students, teachers, and administrators to integrate technology in the same school district. Our hope is that you will think of this book as your coach, because we can't be with you personally. We hope to show you how to integrate the newly embedded tech-related language found within the standards into your everyday curriculum.

In Chapter 1, we address some of the issues that your students face and discuss how important it is to tailor their learning experiences. Today's students are the first generation to truly grow up in the age of the internet, complete with emailing, texting, instant messaging, social networking, tweeting, and blogging. Teaching this new generation of children, teenagers, and young adults can be challenging because of how digital technology has affected their brains and behaviors. The Common Core curriculum has kept this new generation of students in mind, and so will we.

In Chapter 2, we explore the importance of engaging and educating parents. We follow this up with a discussion in Chapter 3 about the equipment you need to teach the standards, and we show you how to address the roadblocks that stand between you and this technology. There are always roadblocks that educators commonly face, and we hope to show you how to get around them effectively so that you—and your students—can succeed. We should also mention that although we are sharing many tools and resources with you, we are not affiliated with any company. The programs, apps, and websites listed in this book are simply those that we feel support the standards.

In Chapter 4, we discuss effective staff development, and we explain in Chapter 5 how the CCSS is organized. Chapter 6 takes a deeper look at the specific standards for the grade level you teach. With these standards in mind, we show you how to begin, offering several classroom-tested lesson ideas in Chapters 7–10 that will ensure your students are satisfying the tech-related benchmarks outlined in the CCSS.

We realize that technology is constantly changing and that digital tools come and go. To make certain that you continue to have the most current resources at your fingertips, visit **our website, (http://tinyurl.com/oexfhcv)**. The website password for the K-2 book is: MCCTSk2. There, you will find an updated list of the apps, software, and websites mentioned in this book.

Let's begin by taking a closer look at today's generation of tech-savvy students and the skills they bring to the classroom.

Chapter 1

Today's Students

A two-year-old taking a selfie? Seven-year-olds tweeting? No doubt about it, today's students come to school knowing more technology than ever before. New educational research suggests that offering a variety of learning opportunities, including lots of technology options, may be the best way to engage today's generation of learners. Educators need to respond to this generation and address its unique learning needs. We believe this so passionately that we think a chapter about this subject is a must in any book about teaching children in the digital age. Technology must be made available to students. Technology must become ubiquitous.

The CCSS are designed to bring school systems into the current century. They are designed with the tech-savvy child in mind. Actually, the standards are designed with their future workplace in mind. That is the driving force behind the technology we see in the standards and why teaching to your students' future needs is extremely important. Please keep this mind as you read this chapter.

Who Are Your Students?

The students you now have in your classroom grew up using digital technology and mass media. According to Debra Szybinski, executive director at New York

University's Faculty Resource Network (http://tinyurl.com/pqwr7va), this generation is:

> ...a generation characterized by some as self-absorbed, attention-deficit-disordered digital addicts who disrespect authority and assume that they can control what, when, and how they learn, and by others as smart, self-assured technology wizards who follow the rules and who are on their way to becoming the powerhouse generation. Clearly, this is a generation like no other, and that has posed an entirely new set of challenges both in and out of the classroom for faculty members and administrators alike.

Some of you are part of this generation. If so, you were the first to truly grow up in the age of the internet: emailing, texting, instant messaging, and social networking. Yet the current generation is ever changing. Those born even 15 years ago did not have technology so pervasive that it was with them 24/7. Many students entering school now are completely immersed in technology outside of school.

Ironically, at many schools, there is a disconnect to students' real lives and their way of learning. Schools are often islands of 20th-century thinking in what is now a 21st-century world. Schools must do a better job of reaching the current generation of students; they need to respond to and address students' unique learning needs. Technology needs to be constantly available to students at school.

What Does This Generation Know and Do?

Many students entering kindergarten now have access to desktop computers, smartphones, tablets, and/or laptops at home. These children begin using all or most of these devices by the time they are three years old. Whether you go to playgroups, parks, or wherever, you're likely to see young children who are working on their parents' tablets or smartphones (or begging to use them!). These students come to us with skills that include (but are not limited to) swiping to work an app; navigating a mouse to play computer games; operating their own electronic devices, such as children's learning tablets, handheld learning devices, and interactive video games; and hunting and pecking on the keyboard to send emails. Also, our tech-savvy students can take videos and photos using a tablet or smartphone, as well as converse with someone by texting, blogging, and messaging. Most have been exposed to the internet and understand that they can find almost any kind of information there.

Because they have so much information at the touch of a button and constant stimulation around them, this generation is often attempting to multitask. It makes sense to them to watch TV, send a text, and find out what the weather will be all at the same time!

Some say that the current generation has hovering parents and a sense of entitlement. While this may be taken as a negative, having parents who are involved with their children and their children's school is a good thing, as it strengthens the home–school connection. Students who have parents who are involved in their academic life can be better students, and they are less afraid to try new things. We, as educators, need to recognize these traits and use them to help students reach their maximum potential.

Being social is very important to the students in this tech-savvy generation. They are certainly the "in-touch" generation, with immediate access to texts, emails, social networking sites, and even the sound of a human voice at the other end of the line. This generation is lost when their smartphone or tablet breaks down; they feel "cut off from the world" when they don't have instant access to the internet.

How Has Technology Affected Students' Minds?

By the time they're in their 20s, today's students will have spent thousands of hours surfing the internet and playing video games. This vast amount of screen time seems to be shortening their attention spans. At a time when their brains are particularly sensitive to outside influences, excessive screen time affects the way they learn and absorb information.

Furthermore, this generation rarely reads books to find information. Online search engines are prevalent in providing all of the information they need quickly, without having to go through a book from cover to cover. With access to an overabundance of information, they need to be skilled hunters who know how to sift through data quickly and efficiently. This new learner doesn't necessarily read from left to right or from beginning to end. Visuals help today's students absorb more information than they do from straight text. Thus, students become better scanners, a useful skill when confronted with masses of online information in a world that's full of noise and multiple stimulations. So, most modern students have learned to block out distractions while they focus on the task at hand.

How Has Technology Affected Behavior?

Because of the constant use of technology, there is less and less face-to-face communication taking place. We all have seen instances of parents and children sitting next to each other without speaking at a restaurant. Instead, they simply sit and quietly engage with their individual tablets or smartphones.

There are many debates about how technology helps or harms the development of a student's thinking. Of course, this depends on what specific technology is used, as well as how and with what frequency it is used in school. Our duty as educators is to decide what technology to use in the classroom and when, because technology influences students' thought processes. We educators need be aware of this effect to guide our students in becoming 21st-century learners.

How Do We Move Beyond the ABCs?

Education has gone through a monumental transformation in the last 20 years. Some changes have greatly improved the way teachers educate, while others are still under evaluation. The great debate between play-based preschool versus learning-based preschool is a case in point. What we have found during our years as teachers is that to progress in the classroom, teachers have to adapt to the times, adopting new techniques while continuing to use time-tested methods. Success in teaching a new generation of students isn't based solely on what educators are teaching them but, rather, how educators are teaching them.

We have seen our share of success stories and our share of students who struggled for reasons that are completely preventable when these students have the right tools. For these highly activity-scheduled and gadget-oriented students, traditional one-size-fits-all teaching is no longer effective. Sitting behind a desk, listening to the teacher talk, and reading from a textbook are completely ineffective. This generation of students needs to be engaged in active and interactive learning to enhance their knowledge. They do not want technology just because it is "cool"; they need technology because it drives their world now and will continue to drive their world in the future. They are looking for something dynamic to make learning come alive—to make it different and interesting every day. Being connected accomplishes that goal.

How Can Educators Succeed in the Digital Age?

Thinking that technology is a new toy that will go away or doesn't have a place in education is no longer an option. We educators need to embrace technology and tap into what our students are already coming to us with, using it to advance their learning. But this technology cannot just be digital worksheets!

This is not always easy, especially when students know more about how to use the technology than many teachers. Therefore, it is our duty to catch up and make sure we know what our students know. This can be done in many different ways; however, the easiest way is to do what they do: pick up tablets or smartphones and start playing with them! Once we have the background skills to know what our students know, we can move forward. We simply need to remember that technology is a tool. And we can use these tools like anything else we use in education—manipulatives in math, novels in reading, and microscopes in science, just to name a few.

Of course, this new reality being imposed on and by the current generation has implications for you as a teacher. It used to be that students conducted research by using books that were from credible publishers, and those books went through rigorous editing and fact checking. This generation uses the internet almost exclusively. If your students get all of their information from the internet, then you must teach them media literacy skills. This skill set has become extremely important in an information age where children need to discern fiction from fact on the internet when, sometimes, we adults have trouble differentiating it for ourselves.

You need to tap into what your students are experiencing every day and use it to your advantage. Many of your current students will work in very social settings but in a different way than previous generations. Let them work often as partners or in groups to create multimedia presentations or digital videos. Because they love to send emails and video chat, let them email, instant message, or video chat with students around the world. This generation is good at multitasking. Allow them to do more things at once, such as opening multiple screens while taking notes on a research paper. Students all know how to use a smartphone, so when on a field trip, let them record a video of what they are seeing. They are used to constant noise and stimulation. Do not make them work quietly at their desks; rather, they should work with hands-on activities like live apps or green-screen technology. Students know at a very young age how to navigate the internet. Let them run to the computer when they have a question instead of asking you, the teacher, for the answer.

We know this new generation of children, teenagers, and young adults can be challenging because of how digital technology has changed their way of learning and behaviors. The following chapters will further address some of these issues and how their learning needs to be specialized, giving more examples of how to integrate technology with the new CCSS. The Common Core curriculum has kept this new generation of students in mind, and so will we.

Chapter 2

Parent Education

The past decade has been financially difficult for schools. States across the country have had to slash education budgets because of downturns in the economy. If your district's budget was not affected by financial cuts, it is among the few. As for the rest of us, we have had to achieve more with less. To make matters even more challenging, we now have new standards that ask schools to immerse students in technology—a very expensive task. Having parents on your side in this budget struggle can be very helpful.

In the years since the CCSS were written and adopted by most states, some attitudes toward the standards have changed. More recently, parents and community members have begun to question them. So it is important, as a teacher, to be proactive in getting the word out about what is going on in your classroom. Work with parents and the community to educate them about CCSS in your state, district, and school. Parents only want what is best for their children, and a little reassurance from you can go a long way.

This reassurance begins with listening to parents. Ask them about their concerns. Answering their questions with facts will help them to better understand why your state adopted the standards.

The following are just a few of the technology concerns that have been raised about the CCSS recently. Knowing about them and other controversial issues allows you to defuse concerns before they become major issues.

Why Do Parents Need to Know about Technology Standards?

You don't need technology to read and you don't need technology to do math—civilizations have been doing both for centuries. Nevertheless, you must admit that technology does help in both areas. If we were still at the turn of the last millennium (1000 AD), we would be hand-copying books. The printing press brought books to the commoner and education to those who wanted to learn. The abacus is fine but hardly as good as a calculator or a computer. Technology marches on so that we can advance, learn more, and pass that knowledge along to the next generation.

The computer revolution of the last century is finally hitting the classroom with the encouragement of the CCSS. Before these standards, the pervasive use of computers was for schools with money or those who could write winning grants. Even so, many schools that were thought to be advanced had not integrated technology into everyday learning. The Common Core is the first set of widely recognized standards to do that. But why do parents need to know about it? There are several reasons.

First, keeping students versed in the fundamentals of technology will enhance your teaching tremendously, and students' parents can help with this at home. Survey parents to see if they have internet access and broadband at home. What kind of equipment do they use—do they have cameras or video capabilities? What do they allow their children to use? Knowing what your students have or do not have at home evens the playing field in the classroom. Encourage parents to teach their children how to use tablets, computers, video cameras, and other mobile devices so students come more prepared to school.

Second, learning doesn't just happen at school. You need to educate parents because they are the main support system for learning away from school. Consistent, clear standards now put forward by CCSS enable more effective learning. Knowing what technology and what software will be used to master these standards greatly assists parents and, in turn, their children. Look at the **Harvard Family Involvement Network of Educators (FINE, http://tinyurl.com/hguh777)** for the latest research and insights on how to get students' parents involved.

Third, technology can instantly link parents to what their children are learning. Knowing assignments, communicating with teachers, and understanding what is expected are all improved with today's technology. There is even an article out there (DeWitt, 2013) about a principal who tried "flipping" parent communication, which you might try too. Whatever you implement is a win-win for you and your students. Take advantage of technology in communication; don't shun it. It will make your life easier.

Finally, we are becoming a smaller, more codependent world. To have a world-class education that keeps our nation and civilization moving forward, all students need to be well versed in the newest technology. That is what the CCSS are all about! The Common Core State Standards Initiative's mission statement affirms, "The standards are designed to be robust and relevant to the real world, reflecting the knowledge and skills that our young people need for success in college and careers" (Council of Chief State School Officers & National Governors Association Center for Best Practices, 2010). In other words, the CCSS is designed for your students' success as adults in the work world, where technology is integral.

Even so, parents must be a part of this endeavor or their children will still struggle to succeed. Involving them is as important to you, as a teacher, as is any other aspect of your students' learning. Do not think of parent education in the CCSS as an add-on—a tool to be used if you have time. Investing in your students' parents and having them on your team benefits you and lessens your load. In a synthesis of studies done on families, communities, and schools, Henderson and Mapp (2002) stated, "Efforts to improve children's performance in school are much more effective if they encompass their families. Regardless of income level or education background, all families can—and often do—support their children's success." (p. 208)

What Issues Do Parents Have with Technology in CCSS?

Parents may ask you about some of the controversial things they are hearing in the news related to the Common Core. One controversy involves a misunderstanding about standards and curriculum. Standards describe what students should know; curriculum is how they get there. For example, even though there is no standard for cursive writing or keyboarding, that doesn't mean it won't be in your school's curriculum. Curriculum is still developed locally. Educate parents who are concerned that they have no control over their child's curriculum—they still have the ability to contribute to what is taught in their local school.

Another controversy centers on test scores from states that adopted the CCSS early on; test scores decreased. Although it may or may not be true in your district, scores quite often decrease when the format of the tests changes. One example is when students go from paper-and-pencil tests to digital assessments. According to Swanson (2013), if your school changed tests, then a result might be decreased scores until students become familiar with the new format. The best way to combat this is to have other digital tests in the classroom throughout the year, to make your students feel more comfortable with the new format.

A common concern we have heard as teachers and as CCSS coaches is that the federal government will be able to collect the data of individual students because of these digital tests. This has been a particularly heightened apprehension recently. The fact is, the U.S. Congress (2010) passed laws that prohibit the creation of a federal database with students' personally identifiable information. Although the law is in place, you should still be vigilant about keeping this sensitive data secure. You are the first line of defense and need to have procedures in place. Please go over your district's privacy policy. If there is none, push hard to make one.

How Can Parents Help with Assessment Technology?

As the teacher, you should help parents and community members understand the types of questions and problems that students are asked to solve on the new digital assessments. During parent nights, open houses, and/or in newsletters, introduce parents to the **Partnership for Assessment of Readiness for College and Careers (PARCC, www.parcconline.org)** and **Smarter Balanced Assessment Consortium (www.smarterbalanced.org) websites**. You can download sample questions to show to parents; and it can also be helpful to put new assessment questions next to old assessment questions so everyone can directly observe the shift.

If your state is going to use the Smarter Balanced test, have parents use the sample questions at the PARCC site to test their children at home. The sample Smarter Balanced test can also be used to prepare for the PARCC test. Both tests' questions are similar and based on the CCSS.

Don't forget the basics. Make sure parents know what kind of equipment the students will be tested on, and have them use similar equipment at home if possible. This will make the device a secondary concern so your students can focus on the test. And send home a sample question weekly so parents can become familiar with the changing assessments. Make sure some of the sample test questions you send home require students to use technology to answer the question, as this will be included on the assessments.

How Can Parents Help Students Meet Technology Standards?

Parents need to see the value of having technologies at home that can help their children achieve more. At the same time, home technology will help you accomplish these new curriculum tasks that, as we teachers know, are daunting, to say the least.

A recent poll by the Leading Education by Advancing Digital (LEAD) Commission found that parents and teachers believe students who lack home access to the internet are at a significant disadvantage. Home access to broadband is viewed as important to learning and doing well in school for the following reasons.

- Home access greatly exceeds anything that your students could ever bring home in their backpacks.

- Home access allows parents to become more involved in their child's schoolwork and allows more effective communication between parent and school, thus promoting greater student success.

- Having home access vastly expands the time your students can learn and explore.

- Home access leads to greater collaborative work, engaging students in online group homework. (This last point dovetails perfectly with many of the new CCSS technology initiatives).

Home access needs to have your active support. At the beginning of the year, run a workshop for parents about the kinds of technology you will be using and why. Teach them how to monitor their children for internet safety as well. You may want to call on your library media specialist or tech specialist to help you if they are available in your school.

Of course, you may teach in an area where parents do not have the funds to have broadband access or technology at home. Following are a few ways to address the issue.

- For homes that have broadband but no computers/tablets, start a program that allows students to check out resources from the school overnight.

- Have after-school clubs or homework help where technology is available.

- Open the school in the evenings for parents and students, providing them access to teachers and to the technology they need.

- Apply for one of many grants available from different levels of government, foundations, and companies to help with your school community's access to technology.

Wherever you teach, parent education is the key to student success with the state standards. Lack of information is one of the main reasons parents are opposed to the CCSS. Being a proactive partner with them will defuse most objections that arise—from parents and from others in the community—and actually create proponents of what is going on in your classroom through this challenging time. Having parents as partners can only help when you are faced with technology needs, such as lack of hardware and software, lack of assistance, and gaps in your students' tech knowledge.

Parent education is only part of the puzzle, however; you must first educate yourself about the CCSS and technology before you can effectively educate anyone. To address this, we have included a chapter on staff development (Chapter 4). But before we explore your professional development options, let's take a closer look at the roadblocks you may encounter on your journey to get technology into your classroom.

Chapter 3

Roadblocks to Technology

Unless your school or district has unlimited funding and gives you completely free reign on your purchases, you have hit roadblocks in your quest for classroom technology. Chances are that you do not have the student technology to become a fully stocked digital age learning environment, but you are not alone. In this chapter, we provide ideas to best use and manage the equipment and software/apps you do have, and we explore ways to get more. It is our hope that when we come to the later chapters on practical ways to integrate your technology into the new Common Core curriculum, you will be better prepared to maximize your resources.

What Are the Roadblocks to Accessibility?

If it is not possible to provide all of your students with tablets or laptops, providing half the class access to this technology is the next best thing. This allows you to work with small groups or pairs of students. Another option is to share technology with the classroom next door to gain at least some time with a full class set of laptops or tablets.

Lack of Funding for 10–12 Laptops/Tablets per Classroom

One option is to have each grade level share a cart of 15 laptops or tablets in addition to a roving cart that any classroom in the school can access. We would suggest grade-level sharing of technology with no more than three sections, as more sections limit student use further. If there are four or more sections in a grade, more carts should be added. This will allow the grade level to have access to at least half a class set. When you need a full class set, use the mobile cart to fill in the gaps. Another way to share additional mobile devices is to divide the 15 laptops or tablets into sets of five for each of three classrooms and then have teachers share devices if a class needs more. You could also place all 15 laptops or tablets on a cart and provide a signup sheet for as-needed use.

Only 4–6 Laptops/Tablets per Classroom

You can use four to six laptops or tablets as a learning center or have half the class double up on them at one time. You can also share with other classrooms near you to get more. You could do this by picking a time every day when two or three classrooms share their laptops or tablets for an allotted amount of time; you could have certain days when you each have them; or you could ask for them informally. The key is easy accessibility.

Computer Lab Limitations

A computer lab with enough computers for all of your students is another great resource, especially if it includes a tech or media center teacher or assistant. This is great because everything is in a set location and there is another knowledgeable teacher available to help. The negative is that you have to sign up for certain times, and everyone must work on the computers at the same time. If you have access to tables in the lab or in a nearby learning space, however, you have the opportunity to do other things with students who have finished their work on the computer, forming smaller work groups as you would in a traditional classroom.

Additional Equipment

How do you choose additional technology to better equip your classroom when your computer budget is already tight or inadequate? Aside from laptops and tablets, it is imperative to have a multimedia projector so that all students can see lesson materials, projects, resources, etc. Other equipment that is valuable includes:

- **Document cameras:** You will use these every day to display written books, worksheets, student work, and the like. Once you have one, you won't know how you got along without one!

- **Interactive whiteboards:** These are great for engaging students, especially during whole-group instruction.

- **Color printer:** Access to a color printer makes student work come to life. (Young children especially love color!)

- **Scanner:** Access to a scanner will help when you wish to scan documents or pictures.

We could have included interactive response systems as well; however, with so many new websites available that can turn your laptops, tablets, or smartphones into interactive technology, buying response systems is no longer necessary.

Some interactive websites that are free (and may offer an upgrade for an affordable fee) are:

- Socrative (www.socrative.com)
- Exit Ticket (http://exitticket.org/)
- Annotate (https://annotate.net)

Keeping Up with Students' State Assessments

Although your students will not be tested in K–2, it is important to understand what they will face beginning in third grade. Different groups developed PARCC and Smarter Balanced to test for college and career readiness starting from Grade 3 onward. Your students may be tested three or four times a year. PARCC and Smarter Balanced (with very few exceptions) are the two main tests that states use to provide teachers the information they need to help students become successful with the Common Core standards. These two assessments are computerized and have certain technology requirements, but they allow traditional paper-and-pencil versions when necessary. (Teachers should still be aware that traditional versions may be phased out eventually.)

We will not address the specifics of network requirements; just know that your school or district will need to meet certain operating system and networking specifications whether they are using the Smarter Balanced or the PARCC assessment. Additionally, your network must be able to address security requirements to keep student information safe. Following are informational sites to help you find what you will need.

- **PARCC technical requirements: (http://tinyurl.com/jmhyrey)**
- **Smarter Balanced technical requirements: (http://tinyurl.com/nuaqy6u)**

How Do We Overcome Software and Hardware Roadblocks?

You cannot benefit from technology if you don't have it. It is also difficult to share it if you don't have enough of it. You need it on time and easily accessible if you truly want to use it seamlessly. This may be the biggest roadblock. We discussed above how you can use different configurations of new or existing hardware in your school. The more pervasive the technology, the easier it will be for you to achieve the goals set forth by the Common Core.

Grants and Foundations

If you don't have enough equipment and/or software, you can apply for grants. While there are more grants available for economically disadvantaged districts, some are accessible to all districts. State and federal grants are available, for example, especially if you can link your needs to the Common Core. The Bill & Melinda Gates Foundation and big companies like Google, Target, and Staples give to schools. Ask your PTA/PTO for money. Many districts have foundations that grant teachers money. You could even ask the PTA/PTO to do a fundraiser for new technology. Following is a list that is by no means complete but offers a great place to start.

GOVERNMENT

- **21st Century Community Learning Centers (http://tinyurl.com/7nx37vb):** This funding is designed to get parents and the community to actively support your work in the classroom.

- **Individuals with Disabilities Education Act (IDEA, (http://tinyurl.com/77b2dwa):** These funds are for students with disabilities.

- **Grants.gov (http://tinyurl.com/k8fybkt):** Search this site for all available federal grants. These grants include:

  - Investing in Innovation Fund (i3)

  - Race to the Top Fund: The government provides grants for Race to the Top specifically for the CCSS.

- Title I, Part A—Improving Basic Programs Operated by Local Educational Agencies

- Title I, Section 1003(g)—School Improvement Grants (SIG)

- Title I—Supplemental Education Services (SES)

- Title I, Part C—Migrant Education

- Title I, Part D—Prevention and Intervention Programs for Children and Youth Who Are Neglected, Delinquent, or At Risk

- Title II—Professional Development

- Title II, Part D—Enhancing Education Through Technology (EETT)

- Title III—English Language Acquisition State Grants

- Title VII, Part A—Indian Education

- **Computers for Learning (http://computersforlearning.gov):** This government program encourages agencies to transfer their used computers and related peripheral equipment directly to schools.

- **State and local money sources:** Look for your state's educational website in our online index at **(http://tinyurl.com/oexfhcv)**.

FOUNDATIONS

Many private foundations offer grants. Following are just a few.

- **Bill & Melinda Gates Foundation (http://tinyurl.com/odwcrra):** This is the largest, private foundation in the world. Its primary aim in the U.S. is to expand educational opportunities and access to information technology.

- **The Foundation Center (http://foundationcenter.org):** This independent, non-profit, information clearinghouse collects information on foundations, corporate giving, and related subjects.

- **Foundations.org (http://tinyurl.com/7sf3c):** This online resource provides an A–Z directory of foundations and grant makers.

- **The NEA Foundation (http://tinyurl.com/or2qc56):** This teacher association gives grants in several areas.

COMPANIES

Many of the companies that manufacture the products we use every day have educational initiatives that offer grants for public schools. Following are just a few.

- **Target (http://tinyurl.com/cdt25kz):** Target offers grants in many areas, including: education, the arts, and public safety.

- **Toshiba (www.toshiba.com/taf/k5.jsp):** Toshiba also offers math and science grants for Grades K–5.

- **Google (http://tinyurl.com/pm9gar4):** Google has several sites dedicated to corporate giving. Google for Nonprofits is a good place to start your search.

- **Microsoft Corporate Citizenship (http://tinyurl.com/p62et7u):** These grants are available for after-school programs.

- **Staples Foundation (www.staplesfoundation.org):** Staples Foundation for Learning teaches, trains and inspires people from around the world by providing educational and job skill opportunities.

- **CenturyLink Clarke M. Williams Foundation's Teachers & Technology Program (http://tinyurl.com/otej8rl):** These grants are designed to help fund projects that advance student success through the innovative use of technology. Teachers in public or private PK–12 schools in CenturyLink's residential service areas are eligible to apply for a Teachers and Technology grant.

OTHER RESOURCES

- **National Charter School Resource Center (http://tinyurl.com/ph2ytng):** This resource website has many links to funding opportunities.

- **eSchool News (www.eschoolnews.com):** This is a great grant resource for K–12 and higher education.

- **Internet@Schools (http://tinyurl.com/nnh5n9d):** This online magazine for education provides a vast list of free resources, grants, and funding.

- **Scholastic (http://tinyurl.com/nd3t97t):** This educational mainstay has many great grant resources too.

Free Software and Apps

Software and app purchases are a challenging roadblock, especially if your district or school doesn't provide enough funding. Fortunately, there are many free resources. Search app stores and type in "free." Free sites, such as Google Docs, are also great places to start. In addition, there are entire sites with free services geared toward the CCSS.

If you are in a small district or a private school, or if you live in a state where funding is limited, follow the money. Go to websites in states and at schools that do have the funds. Look at websites in wealthier school districts near you. Do they have CCSS lessons, activities, and technology ideas that are free to anyone on the internet?

Many states have CCSS resources posted for free! Take advantage of them. For example, New York has many helpful suggestions at **engageNY.org (www.engageny. org/common-core-curriculum)**. Utah has also published a very resourceful Common Core site, which can be found at the **Utah Education Network (UEN, http://tinyurl. com/l2e532)**.

Free software and apps are also available from private companies. These sites usually have ads, or they may want you to purchase add-ons; you and your district will have to judge their value for yourselves. More examples of free applications and websites will be given in the "Practical Ideas" chapters of this book.

What Other Roadblocks Must We Solve?

Systemic educational roadblocks can take many forms, which are often unintended or unavoidable. Here are three common challenges teachers face.

Misguided Policies

Some districts or schools require that all classrooms have the same apps or software. They don't allow teachers to choose what they prefer, and this can be frustrating. If your district wants all software to be the same, you might try explaining why each grade level and each teacher would benefit from using different software, apps, and equipment appropriate to their students' needs.

Some districts implement policies that do not allow teachers to use technology as a tool. Instead, they force teachers to use technology when other mediums or tools make more sense. For example, we discovered a district that required teachers to teach with a tablet 85% of their instructional time. This district even required students to bring tablets to gym class and physical education teachers to use tablets in every class period. School leaders who enforce this kind of policy know very little about infusing technology into the classroom. It would be better to achieve higher technology use through staff development and individual coaching (for example, through the use of this book) than by generating untenable policies that don't actually affect meaningful student learning.

To counter these policies, speak to your principal, go to a technology meeting, or attend a board meeting! Explain that technology is a tool and that the CCSS does not expect you to use technology every second of the day. There is a time and place for technology just as there is a time and place for math manipulatives, a calculator, a book, and even a pencil. Balance is the key. If anything is overused, it (and your effort) is set up for failure.

Parents

Parents will ask the question, "Why do we need new technology?" Have a discussion at PTA/PTO meetings, open house nights, and board meetings about what you will be doing or would like to do with technology. Explain that the CCSS expects everyone to integrate technology, and this is important for today's students. Please refer back to our chapter on parent education (Chapter 2), which has specific suggestions about many of the issues that become parental roadblocks.

Staff Development

Teacher training is so important. You need to have professional development in the area of technology for yourself as well as for your students. If you have a technology coach, great! Spend a lot of time with this coach—set up weekly meetings. They can help you as well as model or co-teach with you. There are many professional development opportunities online as well as off-site in the area of technology. Refer to Chapter 4 to learn how to get staff development outside your district and how to best get around these roadblocks!

How Do You Get the Help You Need?

One of the key components of using technology is getting help. It is very difficult to manage a class of young students who are all trying to use technology at the same time. This is also the case when teachers try to work with a small group while the rest of the class is doing something else on tablets. Inevitably, something goes wrong with someone's computer or students are not sure what to click next. You can teach them to use a few apps or programs if you do it consistently, especially in a self-contained classroom center where students are engaged in independent and self-directed learning activities. However, when you want to expose them to something new or want to change the routine in any way, it is extremely helpful to have another set of hands.

Most elementary classrooms are not fortunate enough to have a full-time aide with them. Therefore, you will need to get more creative. If you have assistants who come to you on a regular basis to help in the classroom, this is a great resource. You can schedule technology use for when they are in the room. This allows greater freedom to work with the whole class—assuming you have enough equipment. You can teach and your assistant can go around the room problem solving. If you work in small groups or at a media center, you each can take a group, doubling your efforts.

If you do not have access to assistants, you might try using parent volunteers. The worst part of using volunteers is inconsistent attendance. However, if you can find a parent or two who is willing to come in on a regular basis, they can be a great help. You will need to find time to train your volunteers, of course, but once you do, most will be savvy enough to pick up what they need to do in class.

If you don't have access to assistants or volunteers, training students is an option. When you are working with a group, have tech-savvy students problem solve technical issues. When you are setting up, they can go around and help other students prepare. We have successfully had student experts as young as first grade. Four or five students can be used to go around the room to help with small tasks, such as printing or finding an app. Training them is fairly easy too. You can do so at recess or during one of their free periods, and it is helpful to have a checklist for them that outlines what you want them to learn. Following are examples of what to put on your checklist.

- How to save

- How to print

- How to find and open software

- How to open apps

- How to carefully handle the equipment

- How to charge devices

- How to distribute equipment (usage policies)

- How to check internet connectivity

- How to use search engines

Make sure that you post passwords where it is easy for students to find them. Forgotten passwords are an annoying occurrence, so having them easily accessible for all will help you manage the situation comfortably.

Another option is to work with your fellow teachers. Consider arranging your schedules so that you each take extra students while the other uses technology with a smaller group. Overseeing fewer students makes technology use much easier to manage.

Create peer groups that have a mix of tech-savvy students and those who struggle with technology. Arrange a time when older students can work with your younger students. Older students like to work with younger ones, and older students can be a big help in classroom management of technology. Even kindergarten classrooms can use technology; it's all in the management.

Although there can be many roadblocks that prohibit you from using classroom technology the way that you would like, there are ways to overcome these challenges. By using the suggestions given in this chapter, we hope you will overcome any roadblocks that lie in your way and that you have most everything you need at your fingertips.

Chapter 4

Staff Development

When technology integration is at its best, a child or a teacher doesn't stop to think that he or she is using a technology tool—it is second nature. And students are often more actively engaged in projects when technology tools are a seamless part of the learning process.

—"What Is Successful Technology Integration?" (Edutopia, 2007)

Without a doubt, today's student comes to school with a strong background and understanding of technology. This generation of tech-savvy students is interested, motivated, and even driven by technology. As you will see, CCSS has explicit technology standards within grade levels. But technology, as a tool, needs to be infused in all other CCSS standards as well. Having a tech-savvy classroom for today's students is the best way to create a 21st-century learning environment.

Truly integrated technology is ever present but invisible. You can use technology as a tool for instruction–as a way to vary the way you present information. You can also provide technology options for students as a way for them to engage in content skills. And students in your class should be given opportunities to create and share their new learning with a myriad of technology tools. The CCSS are not just about presenting information to students; today's students need to be able to plan, reason, analyze, evaluate, and create. Technology integration in today's classroom will do just that—it will not only allow your students to become more engaged in the learning process but empower them to gain a deeper understanding of their learning.

A plethora of articles have been written about the success of CCSS and how good professional development for teachers and staff is a significant key to its success. Technology plays a very valuable role in guiding and fostering this effective professional development, as well as helping to boost current professional-development resources and practices. And technologies that make tools available to teachers on an ongoing basis present a solid jumping-off point for successful classroom integration.

Research has found that sending teachers to workshop-based professional development alone is not very effective. Approximately, 90–100% of teachers participate in workshop-style or in-service training sessions during a school year and through the summer. While workshops can be informational and timely, teachers need opportunities to implement new teaching techniques, not just learn about them. Thus, professional development needs to be ongoing and meaningful to your own professional circumstances. The most effective professional development also uses peer coaches and mentors to implement new learning in class.

How Do You Create a Technology Plan?

You need lots of support and tools to utilize and sustain technology in your classroom. If you do not have a district or school technology director or coach, how do you develop a plan to get yourself (as well as your fellow colleagues) what is needed? You can be the pioneer to get the technology ball rolling.

Following are suggestions to help you begin the journey of infusing technology in your classroom. Although this should not be your task alone, sometimes it falls to a single individual to blaze the trail. Fortunately, there are many online resources that can assist you with creating a technology plan. **Edutopia** is a well-known place to start, offering (among other things) **"Ten Steps to Effective Technology Staff Development" (http://tinyurl.com/oesjsmn)**.

The first step is to put together a technology committee with as many representatives from different buildings and grade levels as you can find. It would be great to include administration staff as well as a district office representative. Parents, students, and outside technology experts can only enhance your committee.

Next, come up with some ways to show how you and your students can use technology in the classroom. Providing specific examples of students working with technology to address the ISTE Standards and the CCSS would be powerful!

Develop a detailed questionnaire for teachers to express their classroom needs, frustrations, and fears. This questionnaire can also serve as a place for teachers to describe what they hope to learn from professional development, including technology goals they would like students to pursue in class.

Ask students to describe the ideal state of technology in their classroom. Ask them how they envision the state of technology in their classroom in one year, two years, five years, and so on. Then place the ideas from this brainstorming session in a public document so everyone on the committee and in the community can see and refer to it.

Lastly, conduct a teacher survey using the **ISTE Standards for Teachers** as a guide **(www.iste.org/standards)**. These standards outline what teachers should know and be able to apply in order to teach effectively and grow professionally. ISTE has organized them into the following five categories:

1. Facilitate and inspire student learning and creativity

2. Design and develop digital-age learning experiences and assessments

3. Model digital-age work and learning

4. Promote and model digital citizenship and responsibility

5. Engage in professional growth and leadership

Each standard has four performance indicators that provide specific, measurable outcomes. You can use them to ascertain teachers' technology comfort level, attitude, and integration use in your school. Answers could be on a scale, such as "proficient enough to teach someone else," "able to hold my own," "a little knowledge," or "scared to death to even try." It may even be helpful to have teachers identify three to five areas that they feel are most important to improving technology within the year. Providing a space for them to write an explanation is also important, as they may not be able to rank themselves on a scale when they can't quantify what they don't know. Writing a paragraph about where they stand with technology might be easier for them. The data you gain from this survey should be shared with your building, other participating schools, the administration, and the district office. And you may want to consider repeating this comfort-level survey several times throughout the year.

Once you've determined the proficiency of staff members, you can enlist their help to create a digital folder of suggested lesson plans, activities, and projects for all to access and use. Your colleagues will not only be able to implement the folder's learning opportunities in their classrooms but add to the folder as they try new things. Something you may want to consider having is a reflection page to accompany any lesson, activity, or project posted. This will help others learn from and refine the ideas as they implement them on their own.

Additionally, your meetings, questionnaires, and survey results will identify teachers, staff members, parents, and administrators who have expertise in specific technology areas. Talk to your principal or district administrators to see if funding is available to pay for the planning time and workshops your experts may wish to lead. (As a rule of thumb, for every hour of professional-development class time, it takes at least two hours of planning.) Opportunities also need to be offered to your experts to advance their professional development. Perhaps you can even find a way to tap into the technology expertise of students, parents, and/or community members by having them lead some of your professional-development workshops. If possible, build in this professional-development/collaboration time at least once a week. Carrying on conversations about the workshops at team meetings, staff meetings, even lunch is a great way to foster and gain interest in what you and your committee are doing.

Even if you are not willing or able to head up a technology committee, there are many things you can do to prepare your classroom for digital-age learning.

What Are Some Staff-Development Ideas?

Be creative in your pursuit of ongoing staff development. If you are pressed for time, observe other teachers who use technology in their classrooms (Ask your principal, department head, or coach to find someone to cover your classroom so you can do this.) If you are fortunate enough to have a coach or staff-development person in your building or district, ask them to set up a weekly meeting with you to work on technology goals. If you do not have a coach, partner up with another teacher or two. Peer coaching, team teaching, peer modeling, or even just conferring with other teachers is a great way to advance your goals, objectives, and outcomes.

There are many conferences and workshops offered throughout the year. Check to see if your district will cover the expenses and provide substitutes so you and your colleagues can attend. Check out the **Bureau of Education & Research (BER) (www. ber.org)**; they are a sponsor of staff-development training for professional educators in the United States and Canada, offering many technology workshops and seminars about how to implement technology with the Common Core. There are also many technology grants offered by businesses. The magazines **Innovation & Tech Today (http://innotechtoday.com)** and **Tech & Learning (www.techlearning.com)** are good places to look for these opportunities.

Ask your principal to provide grade-level time for teachers to look at standards and plan how technology can be used. Then, as a group, develop activities, projects, and lessons that include technology; come up with management strategies for using technology; and (perhaps most important) decide how you are going to assess and evaluate students' learning. This team time is so important for you to brainstorm, share and develop ideas, and gather materials. Summer is also a good time for you and your colleagues to get together to collaborate and develop projects. Check with your district to see if they will provide paid time for your summer work.

Don't forget to share your own successes and those of others. Share disappointments as well so that others can learn from and refine them. Take pictures, write press releases, post on your school's website, and include what you are doing in your parent newsletters and emails. If possible, make a short presentation at a school board meeting. Who knows? You may gain the moral and financial support you're looking for! Share your successes any way you can.

Because needs continually change, keep planning and re-evaluating where you are and where you want to be. Encourage teachers to reach for the stars with their technology needs. Ask students how they feel about using technology and how it has affected their learning. These suggestions will help you and your colleagues get the technology you need.

Where Can You Learn about Staff Development?

There are a multitude of professional-development opportunities out there for technology, either in the workshop/conference format or online (accessible from the comfort of your home or classroom). Some opportunities are free, and some come with a membership fee to use the website or attend organization events. Others are priced per event. Following are a few suggestions.

- **ISTE (iste.org)** has several fantastic staff-development resources, including its Professional Learning Networks (PLNs), which allow you to instantly connect with experts in your field from around the globe **(http://connect.iste.org/home)**. There are many different networks to join (depending on your professional interests) where you can ask questions, learn from colleagues, and get access to exclusive events and professional learning opportunities. ISTE also offers free Strategic Learning Programs with partners like NASA and Verizon, which can be brought to your school or district **(http://bit.ly/1PeJ97t)** In addition, ISTE may have affiliate organizations in your area that provide professional development at seminars and conferences **(iste.org/affiliates)**.

- **EdTechTeacher (http://edtechteacher.org)** is another organization that provides help to teachers and schools wishing to integrate technology to create student-centered, inquiry-based learning environments. They offer keynote presentations, hands-on workshops, online courses, and live webinars for teachers, schools, and school districts—all from your computer! What is nice about EdTechTeacher is that they understand teachers and students because the people leading the professional development have been or still are in the classroom.

- **Education World (www.educationworld.com)** is a complete online resource that offers high-quality lesson plans, classroom materials, information on how to integrate technology in the classroom, as well as articles written by education experts—a great place for you to find and share ideas with other teachers.

- **Discovery Education (www.discoveryeducation.com)** supplies a plethora of digital media that is immersive and engaging, bringing the world into the classroom to give every student a chance to experience fascinating people, places, and events. All of its content is aligned to standards that can be adjusted to support your specific curriculum and classroom instruction, regardless of what technology you have in your room. Discovery Education can help you transition to a digital-age environment and even replace all of your textbooks with digital resources, if that is your ultimate goal.

Because you are reading this book, you have already started your technology journey! And you are not alone in this nationwide endeavor to harness what you didn't know about technology. Kristi Meeuwse, an Apple Distinguished Educator, offers sage advice at her blog, **iTeach with iPads (http://iteachwithipads.net)**, as you begin your exciting learning adventure. You can also read about **"How Kristi Meeuwse Teaches with iPad"** at Apple.com **(http://tinyurl.com/qxzdsbu)**. Following is just a taste of her guidance.

> Wherever you are in your classroom journey, it's important to reflect on where you are and where you've been. It's important to celebrate your successes, no matter how small, and then be willing to move forward and try new things. Daring to imagine the possibilities and being willing to change is not just transforming to your own teaching, it will transform

your classroom in ways you never thought were possible. Today we will do
exciting new things. Let's get to it.

—Kristi Meeuwse (2013, http://tinyurl.com/qf22zo7)

We will continue to give you more resources for staff development in the "Practical
Ideas" chapters (8-10). To learn about staff development in grades other than K-2,
look for the three other titles in this series, as they provide information to help you
differentiate for students at all levels of your class. Before we dive into lesson ideas
for your specific grade and subjects, however, we will discuss how to effectively
read, understand, and use the CCSS standards in the next three chapters.

Chapter 5

Organization of the Standards

S o your state or district has implemented CCSS, and you are asking, "Now what? How can I make this instructional shift, understand these targets, and provide quality instruction for my students?"

You can't make this transition if you don't know your way around the CCSS. So let's focus on the first task: understanding the organization of the standards. While reading this chapter, you might want to explore **"Read the Standards"** on the CCSS website **(http://tinyurl.com/p9zfnwo)** as we discuss the details.

How Are the ELA Standards Organized?

The K-5 English language arts (ELA) standards are divided into six parts (see Figure 5.1), five of which are comprehensive K-12 sections (grey boxes). Then there is one specific content area section for foundational skills in Grades K-5 (white box). (The CCSS website's introduction to the ELA standards has its own **"How to Read the Standards"** section **(http://bit.ly/1ZgEHIa)** that gives more information about organization as well as three appendices of supplemental material.)

FIGURE 5.1. The CCSS English language arts standards

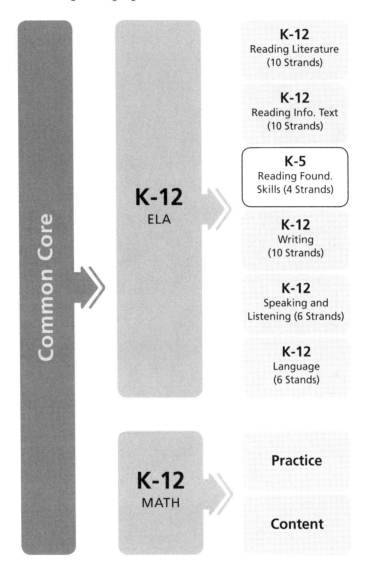

Each section is divided into strands. At the beginning of each strand is a set of College and Career Readiness (CCR) anchor standards, which are the same across all grades and content areas. Take, for example, the first anchor standard illustrated in Figure 5.2: ELA 1 (CCSS.ELA-Literacy.CCRA.R.1). It is the same in kindergarten as it is for a second grader, but the grade-level standard is refined to what the student at each grade level is expected to accomplish within the anchor standard.

FIGURE 5.2. College and Career Readiness (CCR) anchor standard ELA 1 (CCSS.ELALiteracy. CCRA.R.1) with grade-specific standards for kindergarten and Grade 2.

ELA Strand

ELA 1
LITERACY KEY IDEAS AND DETAILS

College and Career Readiness Anchor Standard (CCRA)

ELA 1-CCRA

Read closely to determine what the text says explicitly and to make logical inferences from it; cite specific textual evidence when writing or speaking to support conclusions drawn from text

ELA Grade Specific Standard

Kindergarten (ELA RL.K.1)

With prompting and support, ask and answer questions about key details in a text.

Grade 2 (ELA RL.3.1)

Ask and answer such questions as who, what, where, when, why and how to demonstrate understanding of key details in text.

ELA 1 Anchor Standard: Read closely to determine what the text says explicitly and to make logical inferences from it; cite specific textual evidence when writing or speaking to support conclusions drawn from the text.

ELA 1 Standard in Kindergarten: With prompting and support, ask and answer questions about key details in the text.

ELA 1 Standard in Grade 2: Ask and answer such questions as who, what, where, when, why, and how to demonstrate understanding of key details in the text.

These anchor standards compliment the specific grade-level standards and define the skills and knowledge base that students should have by the end of each grade. The CCR standards are broad, while the grade-level standards provide specificity.

ELA standards focus on the following four areas:

1. Reading

2. Writing

3. Speaking and Listening

4. Language

The reading standards focus on text complexity (the difficulty of what students read), as well as the growth of their comprehension skills. Along with fictional stories and informational text, the CCSS focuses on poetry and dramas too. The writing standards delve into specific text types, reading response, and research. Some writing skills such as the ability to plan, revise, edit, and publish can be applied to most types of writing. Other writing skills are more specific: opinion and argumentation, informational explanatory texts, and narratives. Speaking and listening standards deal with collaboration and flexible communication. In this area, students acquire and refine their oral communication and interpersonal skills, and perhaps demonstrate these skills through formal presentations.

The language standards concentrate on vocabulary, conventions, and effective use. This strand not only incorporates the essential "rules" of standard written and spoken English but also helps students to understand how language functions in different contexts. Making effective choices in meaning and style leads to better comprehension when reading and listening. The vocabulary part of this strand clarifies and/or determines the meaning of unknown and multiple-definition words and phrases by using the appropriate context clues and/or reference materials as needed. This strand also helps students demonstrate an understanding of figurative language, word relationships, and nuances in word meanings. In addition, students will be able to acquire and accurately use a range of general and domain-specific words and phrases in any academic area. (We'll talk more about domains later in this chapter, in the math standards section.)

With the organization in mind, let's learn how you, as an individual teacher, use the CCSS in ELA.

How Do You Find ELA Standards by Subject and Grade?

Since most elementary teachers teach just one grade level, the standards are organized so that you can focus on your specific area. But it is very helpful to look back at the level before you and look ahead to the standards that come next, to put your grade-level curriculum in context. (If you would like to look at a grade not included in this book, please refer to the other titles in this series.)

Using the main "English Language Arts Standards" page on the CCSS website is probably the most efficient way to find your grade- and subject-level standards (www.corestandards.org/ELA-Literacy). If you know what you are looking for, the corresponding reference numbers are useful. Here is a quick introduction:

All standards that relate to literature, informational text, writing, speaking, listening, language, history/social studies, and science & technical begin with "CCSS. ELA-Literacy." The difference comes at the end, with the numbering system.

Let's use the following as an example.

CCSS.ELA-Literacy.RL.2.1

- **CCSS** is the abbreviation for Common Core State Standard.

- **ELA-Literacy** identifies this as an English language arts standard.

- **RL** stands for "reading literature."

- **2** is the grade.

- **1** is the strand.

CCSS.ELA-Literacy.SL.K.5

- **CCSS.ELA-Literacy** represents the same information as in the previous example.

- **SL** means "speaking and listening."

- **K** is the grade.

- **5** is the strand.

But there are standards within standards that are not easily apparent at first glance. For instance, there may be a reading standard that uses historical or science text, or a speaking and listening standard that has a technology component to it. This book focuses on where technology is required in the CCSS, and there is plenty of technology to discuss in ELA and math!

You may be wondering how you will be able to keep all of this straight. After all, we haven't even started talking about math! We invite you to go online to view the math standards (**www.corestandards.org/Math**) as you read this next section.

How Does the Organization of Math Standards Differ?

When you look at the math standards, you will see immediately that they were written by a different group of individuals; they do not integrate other subjects like the ELA standards. Even the mathematical technology standard is separate. And the system of organization is different too. The authors of the math standards also state that the grade-level order can be changed. After the following overview, we will help you sort it all out.

For more than a decade, it has been widely reported that math curriculum in the United States is not even close to being on the same level as math education in high-performing countries. Many feel that math education in the United States needs to become substantially more focused and coherent to improve. To solve this, the CCSS were written to be clear, specific, and rigorous. Not only do the Common Core math standards stress conceptual understanding of key ideas but they continually return to the main organizing principles (place value and properties of operations) to structure those ideas. It is important to note that these new standards address what students should understand and be able to do in their study of mathematics. But asking a student to understand something also means asking a teacher to assess whether a student understands it. Therefore, we need to break apart these standards to enhance readability and to gauge what Common Core math comprehension looks like—so your students will be able to understand and you will be able to assess.

First, you need to understand that in Grades K–5, the standards provide a solid foundation in whole numbers, addition, subtraction, multiplication, division, fractions, and decimals. Also, instead of covering a myriad of topics, your students will be required to immerse themselves in deep comprehension by applying mathematics to problems they have not encountered previously.

The CCSS for math begin with eight Standards for Mathematical Practice (SMP), **(www.corestandards.org/Math/Practice)**, which apply to all grades, K–12. These standards represent ways in which students will be engaged with math content, processes, and proficiencies—longstanding, important practices. The eight SMP are:

1. Make sense of problems and persevere in solving them.

2. Reason abstractly and quantitatively.

3. Construct viable arguments and critique the reasoning of others.

4. Model with mathematics.

5. Use appropriate tools strategically.

6. Attend to precision.

7. Look for and make use of structure.

8. Look for and express regularity in repeated reasoning.

For kindergarten through eighth grade, there are also grade-specific standards. Each contains a number of domains. Domains are larger groups of related standards that are sometimes broken into clusters. Clusters are summarized groups of related standards that fall under the main standard (see the cluster that follows the standard in Figure 5.3). Due to the connected nature of math, you may see closely related clusters in other domains as well. (You can read more about this on the **"How to Read the Grade-Level Standards"** page **(http://bit.ly/1sPykwd)** of the CCSS website's math standards introduction.

The grade-specific domains for K–2 are the following, although for your background information we have indicated that some go beyond the K-2 level:

- Counting and Cardinality (kindergarten only)

- Operations and Algebraic Thinking (K-5)

- Number and Operations in Base Ten (K-5)

- Measurement and Data (K-5)

- Geometry (K-8)

Here is an example of how domains are used to organize the math standards:

CCSS.Math.Content.1.NBT.B.2

- **CCSS** is the abbreviation for Common Core State Standard.

- **Math.Content** identifies that this is a math standard.

- **1.NBT** is the domain (Grade 1—Number and Operations in Base Ten).

- **B.2** is the identifier for a related standard (or cluster) under the main standard—in this case, "Understand place value" (see Figure 5.3).

Now that you know how to identify a math standard and its numbering system, let's look at the following figure to see the way in which this standard is actually presented in this domain.

TABLE 5.3. Example of a standard in the first grade domain of Number and Operations in Base Ten

GRADE	STANDARD	CLUSTER
1	**Understand Place Value**	CCSS.Math.Content.1.NBT.B.2: Understand that the two digits of a two-digit number represent amounts of tens and ones. Understand the following as special cases: • CCSS.Math.Content.1.NBT.B.2.A: 10 can be thought of as a bundle of ten ones—called a "ten." • CCSS.Math.Content.1.NBT.B.2.B: The numbers from 11 to 19 are composed of a ten and one, two, three, four, five, six, seven, eight, or nine ones. • CCSS.Math.Content.1.NBT.B.2.C: The numbers 10, 20, 30, 40, 50, 60, 70, 80, 90 refer to one, two, three, four, five, six, seven, eight, or nine tens (and zero ones).

The standard in Figure 5.3 defines what your students should know and be able to do after you have taught and assessed that standard. Reading and familiarizing yourself with all the standards will go a long way in helping you teach the standards later.

There are also SMPs that are part of the College and Career Readiness (CCR) anchor standards of the ELA. These standards are not overtly assessed but are necessary for you to include in your instruction. SMPs will not be the focus of this book except when they involve technology.

As you can see, math and ELA standards are written and organized very differently. We have tried our best to guide you through these differences, but we do recommend that you explore the resources we have provided here as well as others that we have referenced on **our website (http://tinyurl.com/oexfhcv)**. Here are two great resources that will explain the standards of mathematical practices: **http://tinyurl.com/l3zzsae, http://tinyurl.com/9ndshh6**.

In the next chapter, we discuss technology and how it relates to the CCSS.

Chapter 6

Technology in the Common Core

This chapter focuses on the CCSS English language arts and math standards that have technology-related components written into them, first identifying and then analyzing these standards. This will prepare you for the later chapters, where we offer practical examples of how you can integrate these standards into your curriculum.

As CCSS coaches, we know that there are those of you who are excited about technology, those of you who think it is an annoyance, and those of you who fear it. These new standards will affect all of you because they force your districts and you, as teachers, to use technology more pervasively. Schools will feel pressure to address areas that may have been avoided in the past due to cost or apprehension. If you are a fan of technology, you will welcome the changes; if you are not, you will need to become proficient. You can no longer avoid technology in your classroom.

Where is Technology in the ELA Standards?

The CCSS are designed to prepare students for college, the workforce, and a technology-rich society. And as you learned in the last chapter, the ELA standards have the CCR (College and Career Readiness) anchor standards—reading, writing,

ELA Standards (Grades K–2) in Which Technology Appears

READING (K–2)

- CCR Reading (R) Standard 7 **(http://tinyurl.com/h9n9ek9)**

  - Reading Literature (RL)

  - Reading Informational Text (RI)

- CCR Reading (R) Standard 5 **(http://tinyurl.com/z7cqpqj)**

Note: We will get into more detail about related anchor standard R.5 later in this chapter.

WRITING (K–2)

- CCR Writing (W) Standard 6 **(http://tinyurl.com/zmxfdp8)**

- CCR Writing (W) Standard 8 **(http://tinyurl.com/jercjbv)**

SPEAKING AND LISTENING (K–2)

- CCR Speaking and Listening (SL) Standard 2 **(http://tinyurl.com/gvdrr3g)**

- CCR Speaking and Listening (SL) Standard 5 **(http://tinyurl.com/hrw3bdu)**

LANGUAGE (K–2)

- CCR Language (L) Standard 4 **(http://tinyurl.com/hmu54nx)**

speaking and listening, and language—at their core. Following is a summary of those CCR standards that are embedded with technology in Grades K-2.

Where Is Technology in the Math Standards?

As mentioned in Chapter 5, the math standards are written differently, and the technology standard in math (yes, just one standard) is separate from the rest of the math standards. However, this technology standard is meant to be used ubiquitously. Though many math standards do not overtly say that technology is required, if there is a need for a calculator or statistical analysis using a computer then that is what students should use. In math, the understanding is that these technology tools are used across grade levels and throughout the math standards even though there is only one written standard about it. (Note: This math standard is presented in detail after the grade-specific ELA standards at the end of this chapter.)

What about Using Technology in All Subjects?

Because technology is integrated throughout the CCSS, we should discuss in more depth what this actually means as you go about implementing the curriculum day to day. Though the standards give you specific language, the use of technology has been left wide open. They use terms like "digital tools," "other media," and "both print and digital" to let you, as the teacher, choose what is appropriate to the lesson. The new standards are trying to infuse technology into everyday classroom use, as opposed to having a separate period in a computer lab or someplace you send the students while you are meeting, planning, or collaborating with colleagues. Technology will need to become like the pencil: just another tool to choose from when students need to find the most appropriate one to complete the task at hand.

CCSS strongly encourages project-based lessons and is built to be cross-curricular. Also, Common Core is looking for higher-level thinking, learning, and application. All of these things lead to the use of technology as the most appropriate tool in many situations. They fit very well into P21's (Partnership for 21st Century Learning's) **Framework for 21st Century Learning (http://tinyurl.com/nzvwyen)** and the **ISTE Standards for Students (www.iste.org/standards)**. So if you have been working for some time on lessons that integrate technology and you think you will have to begin again, you will be relieved to know that the new standards are not so different.

How Do You Put ELA Technology Standards into Context?

When you look at the patterns of technology use in the standards, you improve your integration planning and learning achievements with these standards. Let's take a quick look at the technology patterns in the related K–2 standards.

R.7: Although R.7 does not state standards that include technology until the second grade, earlier grades can use it both in preparation for successive grade levels and for differentiation. The standard then continues to develop in subsequent grades comparing text and illustrations in various formats that include technology.

RL.7: This standard begins in kindergarten, comparing illustrations and text, and then grows through the grades, using all types of media to compare, support, and analyze the story's meaning. Essentially, the purpose of the standard is to get meaning from more than the text. Meaning can also come from all the accompanying media and even the format of the story.

RI.7: This is similar to RL.7 but refers to informational text, history, and science and technology. Thus, you must keep in mind informational graphics—maps; photographs; diagrams; charts; and other media in history, science, and technical subjects—and the way in which they augment information or help to solve a problem.

RI.5: Beginning in kindergarten with learning the parts of a book, this standard grows through third grade to an analysis of text structure. Of course, informational text in the 21st century is not only in book form. Getting meaning through the use of electronic menus and graphics in digital media is an important skill that must also be taught.

W.6: This is one of the few anchor standards that is solely technology driven. From kindergarten through high school, students are required to use technology to collaborate with others when writing. Of course, this requires keyboarding skills, but they are not mentioned in the standard until Grade 3.

W.8 Although not explicitly stated in grades K–2, primary teachers should know that CCR W.8 does state technology be used. So digital sources could be taught to younger students who are ready. Technology in this standard is expected from Grade 3 through high school. This writing standard is keying in on the gathering of information, analyzing the information, and avoidance of plagiarism using multiple sources, digital as well as text when writing informative or explanatory works.

SL.2: This standard expects the use of technology from kindergarten through Grade 12. It is a listening standard, but in today's world, all kinds of diverse media are constantly available. Students need to be able to analyze and make decisions about this content.

SL.5: Beginning with the use of pictures when speaking in kindergarten, this standard builds to making strategic use of digital media for presentations in high school. Learning to use media in presentations is critical for college and career readiness.

L.4: This is a very straightforward standard that clarifies the meaning of words at all grade levels. Starting in second grade, students need to know how to find word meanings using not just print but digital dictionaries, glossaries, and thesauruses.

What about Assessment?

You don't begin a trip without an end in mind, and the end that must always be kept in mind with the CCSS is the standardized test your state will be administering. Even though students in K–2 will not be taking part in the national assessments, it is important to prepare them for that eventuality. Whether it is the PARCC or Smarter Balanced assessment, or some other assessment your state is developing, there will certainly be a technology component to it. This, of course, depends on your state and district. In fact, the tests that are being developed will expect students to write short passages using the computer starting in third grade. This is just one example of an assessment (keyboarding) that is not overtly stated as a standard in kindergarten, first grade, or second grade but is expected as a performance outcome in third grade. We, as educators, know you can't start teaching keyboarding in Grade 3 and expect students to be proficient in Grade 3. So it is important to start with the end in mind.

The tests will require some level of competence in selecting and highlighting text, dragging and dropping text, and moving objects on the screen. In the math areas of the test, tools that might be needed for the exam (calculators, rulers, a slide rule) will be available on the screen. Students may need headphones and a microphone to interact during the speaking-and-listening sections, and other multimedia may be used in other parts of the test.

The best way to prepare students is to know in advance the scope of technology they will need to master, but this will not be easy during the first years of rollout. Many things will be changing and many details will still be forthcoming. The tight deadline means your students may not be as fully prepared as you would like them to be. However, your preparation—giving students opportunities to use a myriad of technology as often as possible—will help them to be as ready as they can be for the assessments.

What Are the ELA Standards with Technology?

The following is a listing of where technology appears in the CCSS. The first section contains the anchor standards, and the second section has the more specific grade-level standards. The standards are in order by level so that you can find those that relate to the grade you teach more quickly. The part of the standard that pertains to technology is in boldface type. It is always helpful to look at the standards above and below your level to see where the students have come from and where they are going on their educational journey. Please refer to the other books in this series if you would like to see other grade levels.

READING
CCSS.ELA-Literacy.CCRA.R.7

R.7: Integrate and evaluate content presented in **diverse media and formats**, including visually and quantitatively, as well as in words.

Note R.5 as well: Analyze the structure of texts, including how specific sentences, paragraphs, and larger portions of the text (e.g., a section, chapter, scene, or stanza) relate to each other and the whole.

The R.5 anchor standard does not have any multimedia but does overtly include technology in its informational-text (RI) strand concerning the use of **electronic text** from Grades 1–3 (**RI.1.5**, **RI.2.5**, **RI.3.5**).

WRITING
CCSS ELA-Literacy,CCRA.W.2, CCSS.ELA-Literacy.CCRA.W.6, and CCSS.ELA-Literacy.CCRA.W.8

W.2: Write informative/explanatory texts to examine and convey complex ideas and information clearly and accurately through the effective selection, organization, and analysis of content.

W.6: Use technology, including the internet, to produce and publish writing and to interact and collaborate with others.

W.8: Gather relevant information from multiple print and **digital sources**, assess the credibility and accuracy of each source, and integrate the information while avoiding plagiarism.

SPEAKING AND LISTENING
CCSS.ELA-Literacy.CCRA.SL.2 and CCSS.ELA-Literacy.CCRA.SL.5

SL.2: Integrate and evaluate information presented in **diverse media and formats**, including visually, quantitatively, and orally.

SL.5: Make strategic use of **digital media** and **visual displays** of data to express information and enhance understanding of presentations.

Even when your grade does not have a technology standard included in these main anchor strands (**R.7, W.6, W.8, SL.2, SL.5, L.4**), it is implied that it be used. We have listed here only those that state a technology use. For instance, the first time that **RI.7** overtly states the use of technology is in Grade 4 (**RI.4.7**); but because it is in the anchor standard, it is implied that technology be used in **RI.7** in Grades 1-3 (**RI.1.7, RI.2.7, RI.3.7**) whenever it is appropriate to use it.

What are the ELA Grade-Level Standards with Technology?

Following is where ELA grade-level standards appear in the CCSS (listed by grade). Note the following abbreviations: reading literature (RL), reading informational text (RI), writing (W), speaking and listening (SL), and language (L). We are including Grade 3 to give the technology standards some context. Please refer to the other books in this series to get a sense of the full scope of technology standards, Grades K–12. (Note: as in the preceding section, the part of the standard that pertains to technology is in boldface type.)

KINDERGARTEN

W.K.6: With guidance and support from adults, explore a variety of **digital tools** to produce and publish writing, including collaboration with peers.

SL.K.2: Confirm understanding of a text read aloud or information presented orally or through **other media** by asking and answering questions about key details and requesting clarification if something is not understood.

SL.K.5: Add drawings or other **visual displays** to descriptions as desired to provide additional detail.

GRADE 1

RI.1.5: Know and use various text features (e.g., headings, tables of contents, glossaries, **electronic menus, icons**) to locate key facts or information in a text.

W.1.6: With guidance and support from adults, use a variety of **digital tools** to produce and publish writing, including in collaboration with peers.

SL.1.2: Ask and answer questions about key details in a text read aloud or information presented orally or through **other media**.

SL.1.5: Add drawings or other visual displays to descriptions when appropriate to clarify ideas, thoughts, and feelings.

GRADE 2

RL.2.7: Use information gained from the illustrations and words in a print or **digital text** to demonstrate understanding of its characters, setting, or plot.

RI.2.5: Know and use various text features (e.g., captions, bold print, subheadings, glossaries, indexes, **electronic menus, icons**) to locate key facts or information in a text efficiently.

W.2.6: With guidance and support from adults, use a variety of **digital tools** to produce and publish writing, including in collaboration with peers.

SL.2.2: Recount or describe key ideas or details from a text read aloud or information presented orally or through **other media**.

SL.2.5: Create **audio recordings** of stories or poems; add drawings or other **visual displays** to stories or recounts of experiences when appropriate to clarify ideas, thoughts, and feelings.

L.2.4.e: Use glossaries and beginning dictionaries, both print and **digital**, to determine or clarify the meaning of words and phrases.

GRADE 3

RI.3.5: Use text features and search tools (e.g., **key words, sidebars, hyperlinks**) to locate information relevant to a given topic efficiently.

W.3.6: With guidance and support from adults, **use technology** to produce and publish writing (using **keyboarding skills**) as well as to interact and collaborate with others.

W.3.8: Recall information from experiences or gather information from print and digital sources; take brief notes on sources and sort evidence into provided categories.

SL.3.2: Determine the main ideas and supporting details of a text read aloud or information presented in **diverse media and formats**, including visually, quantitatively, and orally.

SL.3.5: Create engaging **audio recording**s of stories or poems that demonstrate fluid reading at an understandable pace; add **visual displays** when appropriate to emphasize or enhance certain facts or details.

L.3.4.d: Use glossaries or beginning dictionaries, both print and **digital**, to determine or clarify the precise meaning of key words and phrases.

What Is the Math Standard with Technology?

The Standards for Mathematical Practice (SMP) are skills that all of your students should look to develop. As you learned in Chapter 5, there are eight SMP, which are designed to overlay the math content standards. In other words, the math practice standards apply to every one of the math content standards. So, although **MP5** is the only standard that includes technology, it actually means that every math content standard should use the appropriate tools, including tools that use technology.

Following is **MP5**, taken verbatim from the Common Core State Standards website. As in the preceding two sections, any text that pertains to technology is in boldface type.

MATH

MP5: Use appropriate **tools** strategically

Mathematically proficient students consider the available tools when solving a mathematical problem. These tools might include pencil and paper, concrete models, a ruler, a protractor, **a calculator, a spreadsheet, a computer algebra system, a statistical package, or dynamic geometry software**. Proficient students are sufficiently familiar with tools appropriate for their grade or course to make sound decisions about when each of these tools might be helpful, recognizing both the insight to be gained and their limitations. For example, mathematically proficient high school students analyze graphs of functions and solutions generated using a graphing calculator. They detect possible errors by strategically using estimation and other mathematical knowledge. When making mathematical models, they know that technology can enable them to visualize the results of varying assumptions, explore consequences, and compare predictions with data. Mathematically proficient students at various grade levels are able to identify relevant external mathematical resources, such as **digital content** located on a website, and use them to pose or solve problems. They are able to use **technological tools** to explore and deepen their understanding of concepts.

It is important to note the standard's emphasis on using technology pervasively. Keep technology in mind, not only when teaching the standards but in the assessment, as it creates a learning advantage for your students.

We hope you have taken away important information on where technology can be found in the CCSS. In the next chapter, we discuss practical strategies and offer helpful resources so you can begin teaching the CCSS right away.

Chapter 7

Implementing
Practical Ideas

Our world and education is changing rapidly. Without question, one size does not fit all in teaching. We know you work hard to personalize the learning in your classroom to reflect the individual needs, capabilities, and learning styles of your students so they have opportunities to reach their maximum potential. With this in mind, why not create tech-savvy classrooms for today's students?

In this chapter, we address practical ways to use new technology ideas within your classroom. Most of your students already come to school with a strong background in and understanding of technology. They are interested, motivated, and even driven by technology. Having a tech-savvy classroom for today's students is the best way to create a digital-age learning environment.

How and Where Do I Begin?

Whether you are a new teacher, a teacher in the middle of a career, or a veteran teacher with just a few years before retirement, you will begin at the same place in respect to technology. To bring technology into your classrooms and your students into the digital age, you must give up your role at the front of class and let technology be a primary source of information. This journey calls for no longer teaching in the way you've been teaching and instead becoming a facilitator of your classroom and the information presented there. Embrace all of the devices you have ignored or struggled to keep out of your classroom. Introduce yourself to new concepts that may not have existed when you were in school.

First, sign up for as many technology teaching blogs and websites as you can find. One website definitely worth a look is **Power My Learning (powermylearning.org)**. There are many free activities for you to explore, and you can search for lessons by the CCSS. This website also allows you to build classes, assign and monitor student work, and customize playlists for your classroom.

Blogs are becoming an increasingly pervasive and persistent influence in people's lives. They are a great way to allow individual participation in the marketplace of ideas around the world. Teachers have picked up on the creative use of this technology and put the blog to work in the classroom. The education blog can be a powerful and effective tool for students and teachers. **Edutopia** has a wonderful technology blog **(http://tinyurl.com/p33sd7b)**. **Scholastic** also offers a blog for teachers PK–12, **(http://tinyurl.com/oaaycar)** and on a wide variety of educational topics.

Edmodo (edmodo.com) is a free and easy blog for students and teachers to communicate back and forth. We have given you links to all of these resources on **our website (http://tinyurl.com/oexfhcv)**. Teachers can post assignments, and students can respond to the teacher, as well as to each other, either in the classroom or at home. Students also have the ability to post questions to the teacher or one another, if they need help.

What Strategies Can I Use?

Get a routine going. Centers, where students are engaged in independent and self-directed learning activities, are a great way to begin integrating technology in your classroom. All centers can be tied to your curriculum targets, and a couple of them can be technology based. There are a plethora of computer-based games that you can bring to a center rotation. **ScootPad (scootpad.com)** and **DreamBox (dreambox. com)** are two programs that support Common Core and can be used on computers or tablets.

Differentiated math instruction meets the needs of all learners. It consists of whole group, mini lessons, guided math groups, and independent learning stations with a wide variety of activities, and ongoing assessment. Independent learning stations are a great way to infuse technology into your centers. One station with computers and another with games make great rotation centers and are easy to plan for, as well as a great way for students to practice math fluency and target-related games. For more information on how to set up a guided math classroom, check out the book *Guided Math: A Framework for Mathematics Instruction* (2009) by Laney Sammons or view her **guided math slide presentation** online **(www.slideshare.net/ggierhart/guided-math-powerpointbytheauthorofguidedmath)**.

Guided Reading is a key component of Balanced Literacy instruction. The teacher meets with a small group of students, reading and instructing them at their level. Other students are involved in small groups or independent practice that involves reading, writing, or vocabulary. **Reading A-Z (readinga-z.com)** offers many literacy-based books and games that can be used in reading centers. Students can use recording devices to record and listen to themselves reading. You can also listen to their recordings for quick assessment purposes. Reading A-Z also offers **Vocabulary A-Z** and **Science A-Z**. There are many games and activities for these content areas, and this offers you additional rotations for your literacy centers.

Programs and apps, such as Google Docs, Puppet Pals, and Comic Life, are just a few resources you can use to meet standards and bring writing into your literacy rotations. Your students are using technology to be creative.

Flipping the classroom is another great way to integrate technology into your classroom. This teaching model, which uses both online and face-to-face instruction, is transforming education. Flipping is an educational strategy that provides students with the chance to access information within a subject outside of the classroom. Instead of students listening in class to content and then practicing that concept outside of the school day, that traditional practice is flipped. Students work with information whenever it best fits their schedule, and as many times as necessary for learning to occur. Inside the flipped classroom, teachers and students engage in discussion, practice, or experiential learning. By creating online tutorials of your instruction, using some of the tools mentioned in this book, you can spend valuable class time assisting students with homework, conferencing about learning, or simply being available for student questions.

Pick an app or program you are interested in bringing into your classroom. Play and explore. See what the possibilities are for using this technology in your classroom. You and your students can be technology pioneers. Allow your students to problem solve and seek new knowledge on their own and then have them share with you. A great resource to use is **iPad in Education (www.apple.com/education/ipad)**, where you can learn more about how to teach with and use iPads in your classroom. This site from Apple is a great resource—it gives you lots of information about what the iPad is capable of, gives examples of iPad lessons done by other teachers, and offers free apps!

How Do I Determine What Works Best?

Perhaps the next place to look is the **ISTE Standards for Students (www.iste.org/ standards)**. These standards are a great framework to help you plan lessons and projects to support the Common Core technology standards in literacy, math, and critical thinking skills.

The Partnership for 21st Century Skills developed a Framework for 21st Century Learning. This framework identifies key skills known as the 4Cs: Critical Thinking, Collaboration, Communication, and Creativity. Table 7.1 takes those four skills and overlays them with digital resources that you can use in English language arts (ELA). For instance, if you are a second grade teacher and want to use Collaboration in your lesson, you might try any of the seven digital resources suggested to plan your lesson: Google Docs, Popplet, GarageBand, Wixie, Edmodo, wikis, and Google Sites. These are suggestions, but there are many more apps and sites that might also fit well. You might notice that the 4Cs mirror many of the ISTE standards. This table is included to get you to think about how you can include the 4Cs and technology in your daily lesson planning.

TABLE 7.1. How Digital Resources for ELA Fit into the 4 Cs.

GRADE	CRITICAL THINKING	COLLABORATION	COMMUNICATION	CREATIVITY
K-2	Brain Pop Jr. Dreambox Learning ScootPad Reading/Science/A-Z	Wikis Popplet Garage Band Wixie Edmodo Google Docs	Skype Edmodo Explain Everything Show Me Sock Puppets Puppet Pals Garage Band Wixie	Puppet Pals Comic Life Wixie Sock Puppets Garage Band

Being an expert on all of the apps or programs listed in Table 7.1 is not necessary. Start with one you know or find out which ones your students are familiar with and start there. Think about the target or lesson you want to teach. What is the goal? What technology device or app or program will support your teaching? Create an end product to show your students what you expect. Instead of step-by-step teaching of the technology, it is important to let the students explore and discover for themselves, as long as your end product and expectations have been met.

You can also teach yourself about many of the apps or programs available by searching for them online. YouTube also has step-by-step how-to videos for many tech apps and programs. Have your students show what they know by creating samples for you. Save everything you, your colleagues, or your students create, and keep it all in a digital portfolio so you can share them with your students for years to come.

With an active learning environment and providing the tools your students need for 21st-century learning, watch the difference you will make as learning in your classroom skyrockets. All of this new technology is transforming today's classrooms. Social networking and mobile learning are just a few tech-related activities that students and teachers are embracing. The **website for this book (http://tinyurl.com/ oexfhcv)** contains further lists of resources for how to incorporate the technology you have (or want to have) and ways for your students to learn and interact with it. In the following chapters, we further explore the standards for K–2 that incorporate technology, suggest specific applications and strategies, and provide lessons to help students successfully achieve those standards.

Chapter 8

Practical Ideas for Kindergarten

W e realize that you will want to focus on your particular grade or subject when you are planning your lessons and implementing CCSS, so we have organized the Practical Ideas chapters by grade level, then subject. Each grade starts with an overview followed by ELA technology standards with accompanying apps, software, and websites that you can use to help your students have success with that standard. We then continue with the math standard for the grade level, also with accompanying resources. Finally, we have included some sample lessons for each grade level in various subject areas. Although we intend for you to seek your specific grade and subject to help you implement CCSS for your students, please do not disregard other sections of this chapter. To see grades other than K-2, look for our three additional titles in this series, as they could provide information to help you differentiate for students at all levels of your class.

Students entering kindergarten come with a variety of skills, and you will need to establish a baseline of technology proficiency. In the kindergarten standards, technology appears in two areas: writing and speaking/listening. Students will need to begin working with computers, audio recording, video, and tablets to write, listen to stories, watch videos, read, and create pictures using technology. Something for you to keep in mind: Other grades will require your students to have many varied experiences with technology so they are ready for greater challenges.

Writing Resources

> **W.K.6** | WRITING
>
> With guidance and support from adults, explore a variety of **digital tools** to produce and publish writing, including collaboration with peers.

WHEN YOU LOOK AT THE KINDERGARTEN writing standard 6, you realize your students won't be expected to do this on their own. Your class is meant to explore and begin using digital tools with your direct help. The standard specifies "a variety of digital tools." That would mean any and all digital tools at your disposal, from older technology such as videos and tape recorders to newer technologies such as tablets, MP3 players, computers, and whiteboards. Your class should have a good base on which to build. Any word processing software can be used to produce writing and to publish, such as **Microsoft Office (www.office.com), Pages (www.apple.com/mac/pages)**, and **Google Docs (www.google.com/docs/about/)**. Collaboration is another key in this standard. All of the resources in the following list can be used collaboratively. With traditional word processing software, collaboration would be thought of as students partnering, but working independently. Online applications, such as blogs or Google Docs, allow interactive collaboration where students can work together on a piece of writing in real time, whether they are in close proximity or miles apart. You may also want to try something geared more to your younger students. Following are some software options that are more user friendly for the primary grades.

- **Kid Pix (www.kidpix.com):** This software is not free, but students can use it to publish collaborative writing that uses pictures and text. There is a new version called Kid Pix 3D that features more animation. For an alternative, try **TuxPaint (www.tuxpaint.org)**. It is a free online download that is also for primary students and has most of the same features except for stamps or backgrounds.

- **Wixie (Wixie.com)** and **Pixie (www.tech4learning.com/pixie):** This software for purchase uses multimedia, pictures, sound video, and text to create presentations and stories stored on the cloud for mobile access. The apps are free, but there is an online version for schools with more features that has educational pricing.

WEBSITES FOR WRITING

- **Fakebook (www.classtools.net/FB/home-page)** and **My Fakewall (http://tinyurl. com/jhrslv6):** These websites use the popularity of Facebook to encourage writing by creating a Fakebook page or My Fakewall posting to write about characters or historical figures. The site is free.

- **Storybird (Storybird.com):** This free website uses art to inspire storytelling. Students can write, read, share, and print short books.

- **Little Bird Tales (www.littlebirdtales.com):** This website is free. Students can draw original artwork and import pictures to create and write stories. To download a story as a digital movie costs 99 cents, but you can print them free.

- **StoryJumper (StoryJumper.com):** This free site ($24.95 for a hardbound book) gives your students a fun set of tools for writing and illustrating stories that can be shared online.

- **Tikatok (Tikatok.com):** On this free website, there are story starters for Grades K-6 in ELA, science, and social studies that inspire students to write their own books with artwork to share and print. Tikatok StorySpark is the app version, available for $3.

- **Google Earth (www.google.com/earth):** This is a free program and can be used for many purposes at this age level. Students can map their home, find national symbols, and find places about which they are reading, writing, or sharing.

APPS FOR WRITING

- **Explain Everything (www.explaineverything.com):** This $2.99 app uses text, video, pictures, and voice to present whatever your students are asked to create.

- **StoryBuddy 2 (www.tapfuze.com/storybuddy2):** This $3.99 app is easier to use than Explain Everything, but not as versatile, so it may be better to use early in the year to create stories with pictures that can be recorded, printed, and read aloud.

- **Educreations Interactive Whiteboard (www.educreations.com):** This free app is used primarily for teachers to create presentations for their whiteboards, but students can use it to create expository or narrative writing.

Speaking and Listening Resources

SL.K.2	SPEAKING AND LISTENING

Confirm understanding of a text read aloud or information presented orally or through **other media** by asking and answering questions about key details and requesting clarification if something is not understood.

SL.K.5	SPEAKING AND LISTENING

Add drawings or other **visual displays** to descriptions as desired to provide additional detail.

WHAT ARE SOME PRACTICAL IDEAS for using technology in kindergarten speaking and listening? One idea is to have your students read to themselves and record their voice using a tape recorder, smart phone, MP3 player, tablet, or computer. Your class will need to practice asking and answering questions, not just when you read a story or they read to each other, but when they hear or see a story that is an audio recording, video recording, or visual display on a computer. Many websites and apps are free and serve as great storytelling tools. There are also some wonderful resources that you may want to buy, have your school/district acquire, or purchase with help from your PTO/PTA.

There are several options for audio books on CD or ebooks. Program sites such as **Follett Shelf (http://tinyurl.com/oux56og), TeachingBooks (www.teachingbooks. net)**, and **TumbleBooks (www.tumblebooks.com)** (must be purchased) allow you to have access to multiple ebooks that include fiction as well as nonfiction. You can also check out many ebooks at your local library or purchase them from booksellers such as Amazon or Barnes & Noble (especially if you have e-readers). There are some free ebooks out there. **Storylineonline (www.storylineonline.net)** is a free site, donated by the Screen Actors Guild Foundation that has some videos of books read by famous people (including *Harry the Dirty Dog* read by Betty White and *Brave Irene* read by Al Gore). Using the websites, **FreeReadFeed (www.freereadfeed.com)**, or **Freebook Sifter (www.freebooksifter.com)** is a possibility. There are adult titles on these sites, too, so choose carefully. Of course, sites that you pay for give you a much better selection. On **YouTube (www.youtube.com)**, there are many short, free videos that your students can listen to, including folktales, science, and people reading popular books that are in your classroom. Your students can listen and then ask and answer questions.

APPS INCORPORATING STORYTELLING

- **Toontastic (www.launchpadtoys.com):** Students use visuals to tell stories that they can collaborate on and share with others. The app Toontastic Jr. is free with a few backgrounds. Upgrade for $9.99 or purchase a classroom set, discounted depending on the number of students.

- **Explain Everything (www.explaineverything.com):** This $2.99 app uses text, video, pictures, and voice to present whatever your students are asked to create.

- **StoryBuddy 2 (www.tapfuze.com/storybuddy2):** This app, which costs $3.99, is easier to use than Explain Everything, but not as versatile, so it might be better to use early in the year to create stories with pictures that can be recorded, printed, and read aloud.

- **Google Earth (www.google.com/earth):** This is a free program and can be used for many purposes at this age level. Students can map their home, find national symbols, and find places about which they are reading, writing, or sharing.

- **Puppet Pals (http://tinyurl.com/qbgaks2):** This app allows students to create a puppet production using familiar characters to tell or retell a story. It is free, but for $2.99 you can get all the add-ons.

- **Felt Board (www.softwaresmoothie.com):** This app is a virtual felt board that students can use for storytelling. The app costs $2.99.

- **Sock Puppets (http://tinyurl.com/luznt6n):** This free app allows you to create a play with sock puppets. The app records your students' voices and automatically syncs them to the puppets. Get all the extras for $1.99.

- **Kid Pix (www.kidpix.com):** This software does involve cost, but it can be used to publish and collaborate on students' writing using pictures and text. There is a new version that features more animation called Kid Pix 3D. For an alternative, try TuxPaint (www.tuxpaint.org). It is a free online download that is also for primary students and has most of the same features.

- **iBook Author (www.apple.com/ibooks-author):** This app is free and is an amazing way for teachers and/or students to create iBooks. There are galleries, videos, interactive diagrams, 3D objects, mathematical expressions, and much more!

APPS RELATED TO SLIDE PRESENTATIONS

- **Prezi (Prezi.com):** You can sign up for a free educational account and your students can create and share presentations online. Prezi has mind mapping, zoom, and motion, and it can import files. Presentations can be downloaded. A Prezi viewer app is available.

- **Wixie (Wixie.com) and Pixie (www.tech4learning.com/pixie):** This software (for purchase) uses multimedia, pictures, sound video, and text to create presentations and stories stored on the cloud for mobile access. The apps are free, but there is an online version for schools with more features that has educational pricing.

WEBSITES RELATED TO SPEAKING AND LISTENING

- **Little Bird Tales (www.littlebirdtales.com):** This website is free. Students can draw original artwork and import pictures to create and write stories. To download as a digital movie costs 99 cents, but you can print them free.

- **RealtimeBoard (www.realtimeboard.com):** This website is an endless whiteboard, which allows you to enhance your classroom lessons, create school projects, work collaboratively with team members, and so much more. There is a free education version, when you use a school email address. Upgrades are also available.

Math Resources

MP5	MATH
Use appropriate **tools** strategically.	

THERE ARE TWO MAIN SETS of standards, processes and practices, for the Common Core Math standards. First, you have the math targets, written similarly to ELA (Counting and Cardinality; Operations & Algebraic Thinking; Number & Operation in Base Ten; Measurement & Data; and Geometry). While you work with students on mathematical processes such as counting and cardinality in kindergarten, you need to teach them how to apply the Standards for Mathematical Practices, such as problem solving and precision, to those processes. One practice, the only one that includes technology, is mathematical practice 5, "Use appropriate tools strategically."

Following is the explanation CCSS provides for **MP5**. As this is the standard explanation for grades K–12, it does include references to higher grades.

Mathematically proficient students consider the available tools when solving a mathematical problem. These tools might include pencil and paper, concrete models, a ruler, a protractor, **a calculator, a spreadsheet, a computer algebra system, a statistical package, or dynamic geometry software.** Proficient students are sufficiently familiar with tools appropriate for their grade or course to make sound decisions about when each of these tools might be helpful, recognizing both the insight to be gained and their limitations. For example, mathematically proficient high school students analyze graphs of functions and solutions generated using a graphing calculator. They detect possible errors by strategically using estimation and other mathematical knowledge. When making mathematical models, they know that technology can enable them to visualize the results of varying assumptions, explore consequences, and compare predictions with data. Mathematically proficient students at various grade levels are able to identify relevant external mathematical resources, such as **digital content** located on a website, and use them to pose or solve problems. They are able to use **technological tools** to explore and deepen their understanding of concepts.

Because this description does not give examples for all grades, we have provided a list of appropriate apps, websites, software, and lessons that will help translate this standard for kindergarten.

Your students will need to begin using technology as a tool to help them strengthen their math skills. That is essentially what this math standard, the only one that explicitly includes technology, states. Using technology as a mathematical practice tool can be interpreted in many different ways. In any case, students should use technology as a math tool as much as possible. Fortunately, there are many math programs, websites, and apps to choose from. The best of them have students learning in creative ways and are not just electronic worksheets. They automatically adapt to the students' skill levels, and they give you data that tells you where students are in their learning and what they need to effectively continue. Of course, these usually do not come free. Following are many good math resources. The free resources (many with ads) are often less interesting to students and not as well organized. They don't give you the feedback you need. However, you must make the decision about what is best for your circumstances and budget.

WEBSITES FOR MATH

- **ScootPad (scootpad.com):** This is a web-based math site that is totally customizable for individual students. It adapts to the student and keeps the teacher in the loop with multiple reports. It is completely aligned to the CCSS. The price for a class varies from $5 to $20/month.

- **BrainPOP Jr. (www.brainpop.com):** This site offers top-notch educational videos for elementary school teachers. However, most are Flash and don't work for iPad unless you have an additional Flash player app. Price is $85 to $145.

- **IXL (www.ixl.com/math/):** This online site features adaptive individualized math through gameplay. It gives students immediate feedback and covers many skills, despite its emphasis on drills. It has levels from prekindergarten to Grade 8. The class price is $199/year.

- **BBC: Schools: Numeracy (http://tinyurl.com/y9k7xj):** This free site has many great online interactive math products that are free without ads and organized by skill, although you won't be able to track your students' progress.

- **Prodigy (www.prodigygame.com):** This is an online adaptive math practice site wrapped in role-playing adventure from Canada. The base price is free with optional paid upgrades with membership.

- **PBS LearningMedia (www.pbslearningmedia.org):** This site is a great source for classroom-ready, free digital resources. There are resources here for every subject, including math.

- **PrimaryGames (http://tinyurl.com/72ojhan), Coolmath-Games (www.coolmath-games.com), SoftSchools (www.softschools.com),** and **Sheppard Software (http://tinyurl.com/ccrxoa)** are several sites that have free math games that cover all math topics at each grade level. However, these sites have ads, are not able to keep track of a student's success rate, and are not generally self-adaptive to a student's skill level.

- **Count Us In (www.abc.net.au/countusin):** This is a free website by ABC Australia that has some great primary activities and resources for your students, but it is not self-adaptive.

- **Kindersite (www.kindersite.org):** A free site that does not have ads, but you will need to search through the games to find those appropriate to the skill you need. Moreover, it will not keep track of students' success rate. The games are not adaptive to skill level.

APPS FOR MATH

- **Explain Everything (www.explaineverything.com):** This $2.99 app uses text, video, pictures, and voice to present whatever your students are asked to create. It is very useful for explaining math concepts and creating visual math.

- **Bugs and Bubbles (http://tinyurl.com/hdr3bxe):** Fascinating graphics engage

PK-1 students as they practice pre-reading and STEM skills. This app also adapts to users' level of math skill. Cost is $2.99.

- **Todo K-2 Math Practice (http://tinyurl.com/pm6tmlk):** One arithmetic app fulfills the needs of many learners in K-2, and the app is free.

- **Teachley: Addimal Adventure (http://tinyurl.com/p2ub7eo):** This is a well-designed app that concentrates on K-2 addition using learning research and strategies through a fun, graphical set of games. It can track students' progress and their methods of learning. Free.

- **Elmo Loves 123s (http://tinyurl.com/na72o4b):** This app is for iPad and Android. Sesame Street sets the standard for teaching numbers with characters kids love. The app price is $4.99.

- **Love to Count by Pirate Trio (www.nextisgreat.com):** Built for PK-2 students, this app has hundreds of tasks and swashbuckling fun for new math learners. The price for the app is $3.99.

- **Motion Math: Hungry Fish (http://tinyurl.com/pnulzgc):** Six games build mental math skills and promote fact fluency with a fish hungry for numbers. Cost is $1.99.

WEBSITES WITH APPS FOR MATH

- **Sumdog (www.sumdog.com):** This is an online adaptive set of math games. In addition, there are apps available for tablets and minis. It is free, but you can get more programs, reports, and so on if you purchase an upgrade. It is not necessary to upgrade to use the site.

- **DreamBox Learning Math (www.dreambox.com):** This is an individualized, adaptive game-based math program that keeps kids coming back for more. Available online or through an app. Cost is $12.95/month (home) or $25/month (school). It is less per student if it's packaged with other classes, a whole school, or district.

DIGITAL MATH GAMES

Many studies in recent years have shown how math games can increase student learning. Also, a survey (http://tinyurl.com/pqms3nj) released in late summer 2014 from the Games and Learning Publishing Council indicates that the use of digital games in the classroom is becoming more popular with teachers. The survey indicates that 55% of teachers who responded have students play digital games in their classroom weekly.

With this research and study in mind, the week of the 100th day of school is a perfect time for your students to do some fun activities on the computer that are related to the number 100. First, watch the BrainPOP, Jr. video "One Hundred" on the interactive whiteboard. Then, have students try to identify the mystery word on a hundred chart and a mystery picture by connecting the dots from 1 to 100. Following are some websites that offer fun 100th day of school activities to try at the computer.

- **Splat Square (http://tinyurl.com/38exsd):** This is a hundred grid game, which can be played electronically or printed out. Teacher "calls out" a specific number as the target and students find the number and "splat" it.

- **Mathwire (mathwire.com):** Many standards-based math activities for the 100th day of school!

- **Give the Dog a Bone (http://tinyurl.com/btnmg):** An interactive game where students try to find the 10 hidden bones on the hundreds chart in less than a minute.

- **100 Snowballs (http://tinyurl.com/6jyuvuk):** Another interactive activity that gives students the chance to play and have fun in the snow! Students click and drag snowballs around in the snow, creating any scene they desire—as long as they use only 100 snowballs!

- **TVO Kids (http://tinyurl.com/pnmu89s):** Many 100th day of school interactive math games and perfect for differentiating! Games are in two categories: 2 to 5 years of age; and 11 and under. Many other math and reading games are on this site as well.

Literacy Lessons

Cross-curriculum planning is encouraged with the CCSS by using ELA standards in history, science, and technical subjects. Getting through all of the standards you need in kindergarten is very difficult in the time given. The key to planning with the CCSS is to teach multiple standards in one lesson. We strongly encourage doing this when possible. With the following list of sample lessons for kindergarten, we hope you will be inspired to become effective technology lesson planners. The following two sample lessons address CCSS ELA standards.

SENTENCE WRITING

This first lesson uses Puppet Pals or Sock Puppets on the iPad. The students' assignment is to write a narrative sentence. Using Puppet Pals or Sock Puppets, students choose their characters and backdrop. Next, they record their narrative while moving the puppets. Students choose from one of three writing prompts:

1. Write about your favorite family vacation. Where did you go? Who was there? Why was it your favorite?

2. Write about your favorite birthday party. How old were you? Why was it your favorite?

3. Write about your favorite holiday that you and your family celebrate. Why is it your favorite? What are your family traditions?

The students' digital puppet shows can then be presented and shared in class. This simple lesson's primary focus satisfies **W.K.6**, which explores a variety of digital tools to produce and publish writing, including collaboration. Also satisfied is **SL.K.2** by asking and answering questions in text read in other media and **SL.K.5** by including visual displays.

CLASS MASCOTS

Kindergarten teachers we know each have a class mascot (the cow class, the penguin class, etc.). One teacher uses the class mascot (other objects can be used as well) to demonstrate that a preposition is anywhere the class mascot can go. The teacher used a digital camera to take pictures of the mascot on the table, in a lunch box, sitting by the computer, sitting with a friend, etc. Choose any favorite media tool for composing a digital book about your class mascot and its adventures with prepositions. Students help create the book by dictating sentences for each picture and preposition. This particular teacher chose iBook Author to compose the book. She has the class book stored on her tablets. During center time, students work with this book and record themselves (on the tablet) echo reading the preposition pages. Other teachers loved this idea so much they copied it, but used a different media tool for composing a book. One used Puppet Pals, while another used Wixie. There are many possibilities for this lesson. The primary focus for this lesson satisfies **W.K.6**, which explores a variety of digital tools to produce and publish writing, and collaboration. Also satisfied is **SL.K.2**, by choral reading the preposition sentences. Confirming understanding is checked by having students record their choral reading. Teachers can then not only listen to the individual choral readings, but check for understanding individually or across the whole class.

Social Studies/Science Lessons

The following sample lessons address CCSS ELA standards and teach lessons based on national standards in social studies and science.

USING DIGITAL TOOLS

Kindergarten teachers tell us they love to use Google Earth to reinforce classroom learning whenever possible. For example, when the class is discussing American symbols (like the White House or the Statue of Liberty), they visit them via Google Earth. Images are often in 3D, which really gets the students' interest. The teachers then have students use Puppet Pals to illustrate their learning. With help from an adult, students pick a background and find the symbols they were learning. Next, they narrate a brief description of what the symbol is and where it is located. Students can then take a picture of one of their Puppet Pal pages using a tablet, as well as print a page to hang in the hall. Then, using a reader like **i-nigma Reader (www.i-nigma.com/i-nigmahp.html)** or **QR Code Generator (www.qr-code-generator.com)**, the teacher assigns a QR code to the printed page. Students' work can be hung in the hallway. Anyone passing by can use their smartphone with a QR reader to see the students' entire projects. This lesson also satisfies **W.K.6** by exploring a variety of digital tools to produce and publish writing, including collaboration, as well as **SL.K.2**, by asking and answering questions in text read in other media, and **SL.K.5**, by including visual displays.

WEATHER ACTIVITIES

Most kindergarten teachers discuss weather during daily calendar time. Several times a year teachers guide the students in a discussion about the seasons of the year, as well as types of clothing to wear. During the discussion, students name clothing associated with each season. The teacher lists clothing words on the interactive whiteboard as students name them. Students are then led in a discussion of how to sort the words into categories and they are asked to explain their choices. The teacher writes the word on a chart divided into four sections labeled, fall, winter, spring, summer. Following the sorting activity, students write about their favorite season using words from the interactive whiteboard. Teachers can choose their favorite media tool (Wixie, Pixie, Kid Pix, Little Bird Tales, etc.) to have students write their story about their favorite season. Students include drawings and phonetically spelled words to add meaning to their writing. Students then record themselves reading their stories to the class. Presentations by students can also be done in front of the class. This activity can be done several times a year. Students can see and compare what they wrote previously by storing presentations on desktops or in classroom ebook shelves. This activity can also be differentiated in many ways. For example, phonetically spelled words can become simple sentences; pictures can be labeled; and students can work collaboratively or individually. This simple lesson's primary focus satisfies **W.K.6**, which explores a variety of digital tools to produce and publish writing, including collaboration. Also satisfied is **SL.K.2**, by reading aloud (and recording) about their favorite season, and **SL.K.5**, by including visual displays to describe and add detail to their story.

Math Lessons

The following two sample lessons address the CCSS math standard **MP5**.

SHAPES

A math example when the class is discussing shapes has students use technology tools to explore and deepen understanding of concepts. With adults, students venture around the school finding examples of squares, circles, and triangles. Students draw them using Explain Everything. Next, they record what shape they saw and how they know it is a particular shape. Depending on how savvy students are with a tablet, they can take a picture of what they find, import to Explain Everything, and record information about a shape (four equal sides, etc.) A colleague reported that her kindergarten students are able to snap pictures using a tablet and upload them to Explain Everything. However, students needed time to practice this task. This is a great way to satisfy standard **MP5**. In addition, this lesson satisfies **SL.K.2** by asking and answering math questions in text read in other media and **SL.K.5** by including visual displays.

ITCHY ITCHY CHICKEN POX

To help teach counting and cardinality, teachers start this project by reading *Itchy, Itchy Chicken Pox*. Teachers lead students through the book counting the chicken-pox on each page. You actually can read the book and count for several days, each day discussing how you can represent 7 chicken-pox (7 red dots, 4 dots plus 3 dots, etc.). Next, take a digital picture of each student's face in your classroom. Remind them you will be making a book of them with chicken-pox. Did the boy look happy in the story? Choose any favorite media tool for composing a digital book (Wixie, eBook, iBook Author, etc.) and download the individual pictures of your class. Each student's face will be one page. Under each, face type the sentence, "Look at me! I have _____ chickenpox!" Make sure the media tool you choose allows students to write/draw on their picture. Discuss with your students the range of chickenpox on the boy's face in the book. Discuss with them the possibilities they have for drawing chickenpox on their faces. Each student will then have a turn to draw a number of red chickenpox dots on their face. In the blank, students write how many chicken-pox they have. Below that, students can write their name. Encourage differentiation here! Any student who can write their number other than in numeral form should be encouraged to do so—for example, 4 + 3; 3 × 2; VIII (yes, even Roman numerals); or in another language! To go one step further, you may wish to have students record their voices, saying how many chickenpox they have. The teacher can also show the digital book to the class and ask questions, such as "How many chicken-pox does ____ have? How do you know?" This digital book can then be stored on your desktop or ebook shelf for students to come back to all year long. This counting lesson also satisfies **W.K.6**, exploring a variety of digital tools to produce and publish writing, including collaboration (individually and whole class), as well as **SL.K.2** by asking and answering questions in text read in other media and **SL.K.5** by including visual displays. This is a great way to satisfy standard **MP5**.

A Final Note

It is clear that as students progress through the primary grades, they are establishing their baseline of proficiency in technology. This will definitely enhance their experiences with technology in the upper grades, as well as satisfy the CCSS performance standards at the K–2 level. We hope that you found the resources and lesson ideas presented in this chapter useful and that they are easy to adapt to your class.

You will find more resources online at **our website (http://tinyurl.com/oexfhcv)**, which may be helpful to you and could be useful as you look to differentiate your instruction. Visit our online site for updated information about this book. To learn more about meeting technology standards found within the CCSS in other grades, look for our three additional titles in this series.

Chapter 9

Practical Ideas for First Grade

We realize that you will want to focus on your particular grade or subject when you are planning your lessons and implementing CCSS, so we have organized the Practical Ideas chapters by grade level, then subject. Each grade starts with an overview followed by ELA technology standards with accompanying apps, software, and websites that you can use to help your students have success with that standard. We then continue with the math standard for the grade level, also with accompanying resources. Finally, we have included some sample lessons for each grade level in various subject areas. Although we intend for you to seek your specific grade and subject to help you implement CCSS for your students, please do not disregard other sections of this chapter. To see grades other than K–2, look for our three additional titles in this series, as they could provide information to help you differentiate for students at all levels of your class.

Students in first grade are expected to accomplish many of the same standards as kindergarteners. Three of the four standards are very similar. Therefore, your students coming into first grade should have a background in many of the standards that feature technology in your first grade classroom. The only difference is the first standard listed next (**RI.1.5**). The reading standard has added a technology component to first grade (electronic menus, icons) that in kindergarten had only basic text features (headings, tables of contents, glossaries).

Reading Resources

> **RI.1.5** | READING INFORMATION
>
> Know and use various text features (e.g., headings, tables of contents, glossaries, **electronic menus, icons**) to locate key facts or information in a text.

THIS MAY BE YOUR STUDENTS' FIRST foray into using specific features in informational text that might be digital. In kindergarten, your students were taught common parts of a book. Now they will be adding electronic menus and icons they might see in digital books, internet pages, and software. Students will need to learn how to navigate and interpret software and internet menus. Additionally, you will need to make sure they know the function of most major icons. Unfortunately, there are few resources currently available that specifically teach this concept. That does not mean you will have a problem teaching this standard. It is easily included in everyday lessons. When you are introducing a new piece of software or app to the class, make this a part of the lesson. When you look at an internet page, email page, or word processing document as a class, discuss the common menu choices and what each does.

Following are some practical ideas for teaching digital text features in first grade informational text.

- Every time you introduce a new app or piece of software, you should point out the similarities in the menu options, such as where Open, Print, Save, and so on, are usually found.

- Many icons have become standardized in software. How do these help them find information on a page more easily?

  - A printer icon for print

  - A magnifying glass for search and zoom in and out

  - Arrows for next or forward, last, or backspace

  - Rounded arrows for undo and redo, etc.

- Discuss why these icons were chosen, discuss their meaning, and make a game of finding them in new programs.

- Tell students how to find and use the spelling help in many programs.

- Discuss what "cut" and "paste" are in digital terms.

- Discuss text features and formats, such as font types, boldfacing, underlining, resizing text, and why they would use different sizes and boldness for headings and subheadings. How do these help them find information on a page more easily?

- You may want to differentiate for your more capable students by discussing tabs and paragraphs.

Writing Resources

W.1.6	WRITING

With guidance and support from adults, use a variety of **digital tools** to produce and publish writing, including in collaboration with peers.

YOUR FIRST GRADERS WILL BE coming to you with some background in writing using digital resources. To continue this and augment their learning, you should give those experiences with as many varied digital tools as possible. This would include computers, tablets, and minis using the internet, software, and apps. Even if you only have just one type of digital tool, you can still vary activities with some of the free sites listed here. Please remember that part of this standard includes collaboration, which the following applications we list help to facilitate.

SOFTWARE

- **Kid Pix (www.kidpix.com):** This software is not free, but it can be used to publish and collaborate on students' writing using pictures and text. There is a new version that features more animation called Kid Pix 3D. For an alternative, try **Tux Paint (www.tuxpaint.org)**. It is a free online download, which is also for primary students and has most of the same features.

- **Wixie (www.wixie.com)** and **Pixie (www.tech4learning.com/pixie):** This software (for purchase) uses multimedia, pictures, sound video, and text to create presentations and stories stored on the cloud for mobile access. The apps are free, but there is an online version for schools with more features that has educational pricing.

WEBSITES FOR WRITING

- **Fakebook (www.classtools.net/FB/home-page)** and **My Fakewall (http://tinyurl.com/jhrslv6):** These websites use the popularity of Facebook to encourage writing by creating a Fakebook page or wall posting to write about characters or historical figures. The site is free.

- **PebbleGo (www.pebblego.com):** This website from the publisher Capstone has taken their books and made them digital. They include print, pictures, video, and audio and are great for researching at the K–3 level. Articles are leveled, and the site is interactive. The cost is steep at $395 to $995/year, depending on what package you choose.

- **Storybird (storybird.com):** This free website uses art to inspire storytelling. Students can write, read, share, and print short books.

- **StoryJumper (storyjumper.com):** This free site ($24.95 for a hardbound book) gives your students a fun set of tools for writing and illustrating stories that can be shared online.

- **Tikatok (www.tikatok.com):** On this website, there are story starters for Grades K–6 in ELA, science, and social studies that inspire students to write their own books with artwork to share and print. Classroom price is $19/year. Tikatok Story Spark is the app that you can purchase for $3.

- **Little Bird Tales (www.littlebirdtales.com):** This website is free. Students can draw original artwork and import pictures to create and write stories. To download as a short video (MPG4) is 99 cents. However, you can print stories free.

- **Google Earth (www.google.com/earth):** Students at this age can use this free program for many varied purposes, such as mapping their home, finding national symbols, and finding places about which they are reading, writing, or sharing.

APPS FOR WRITING

- **Explain Everything (www.explaineverything.com):** This $2.99 app uses text, video, pictures, and voice to present whatever your students are asked to create.

- **StoryBuddy 2 (www.tapfuze.com/storybuddy2/):** This app is easier to use than Explain Everything, but not as versatile, so it might be better to use early in the year to create stories with pictures that can be recorded, printed, and read aloud. $3.99

- **Educreations Interactive Whiteboard (www.educreations.com):** This free app is used primarily for teachers to create presentations for their whiteboards, but can be used by students to create expository or narrative writing.

- **Puppet Pals (http://tinyurl.com/qbgaks2):** This app allows students to create a puppet production using familiar characters to tell or retell a story. It is free, but for $2.99 you can get all the add-ons.

Speaking and Listening Resources

SL.1.2	SPEAKING AND LISTENING

Ask and answer questions about key details in a text read aloud or information presented orally or through **other media**.

SL.1.5	SPEAKING AND LISTENING

Add drawings or other **visual displays** to descriptions when appropriate to clarify ideas, thoughts, and feelings.

YOUR FIRST GRADE STUDENTS HAVE many opportunities for speaking and listening when partnered up in different activities, including reading to each other, but this section is focusing on using technology. The standards require your students to be able to share through media and create digital pictures or drawings to help them explain something. The simplest way to help them meet this standard is to have your students read to themselves and record their voices using a tape recorder, smart phone, MP3 player, tablet, or computer. Then have other students listen to the recordings and ask and answer questions.

There are a variety of options for audio books on CD or ebooks: Program sites such as **Follett Shelf (http://tinyurl.com/oux56og), TeachingBooks (www.teachingbooks. com),** and **TumbleBooks (www.tumblebooks.net)** (must be purchased) allow you to have access to multiple ebooks that include fiction as well as nonfiction. You can also check out many ebooks at your local library or purchase them from booksellers such as Amazon or Barnes & Noble (especially if you have e-readers). There are some free ebooks out there. **Storylineonline (www.storylineonline.net)** is a free site, donated by the Screen Actors Guild Foundation, that has some videos of books read by famous people (including *Harry the Dirty Dog* read by Betty White and *Brave Irene* read by Al Gore). Using the sites, **FreeReadFeed (www.freereadfeed.com),** or **Freebook Sifter (www.freebooksifter.com)** is a possibility. There are adult titles on these sites, too, so choose carefully. Of course, sites that you pay for give you a much better selection.

Following are some practical ideas for using technology in first grade speaking and listening.

- **YouTube (www.youtube.com):** There are many short, free videos that your students can listen to, including folktales, science, and people reading popular books that are in your classroom. Your students can listen and then ask and answer questions.

- **BrainPOP Jr. (www.brainpop.com):** This is a great resource to use for many areas of your curriculum. There are great video animations, and it comes with a questions and answer section. This does cost money, but it is well worth the significant price if you can find the funds. Price is $85 to $145.

- **Wixie (www.wixie.com)** and **Pixie (www.tech4learning.com/pixie):** This software (for purchase) uses multimedia, pictures, sound video, and text to create presentations and stories stored on the cloud for mobile access.

- **RealtimeBoard (www.realtimeboard.com):** This endless whiteboard allows you to enhance your classroom lessons, create school projects, work collaboratively with team members, and so much more. There is a free education version, when you use a school email address. Upgrades are also available.

- **Prezi (www.prezi.com):** You can sign up for a free educational account and your students can create and share presentations online. Prezi has mind-mapping, zoom, and motion, and it can import files. Presentations can be downloaded. There is a Prezi viewer app available.

APPS FOR STORYTELLING

- **Toontastic (www.launchpadtoys.com):** Students use visuals to tell stories that they can collaborate on and share with others. The app Toontastic Jr. is free with a few backgrounds. Upgrade for $9.99 or purchase a classroom set, discounted depending on the number of students.

- **Explain Everything (www.explaineverything.com):** This $2.99 app uses text, video, pictures, and voice to present whatever your students are asked to create.

- **StoryBuddy 2 (www.tapfuze.com/storybuddy2/):** This app, which costs $3.99, is easier to use than Explain Everything, but not as versatile. You can use it to create stories with pictures that can be recorded, printed, and read aloud.

- **Puppet Pals (http://tinyurl.com/qbgaks2):** This app allows students to create a puppet production using familiar characters to tell or retell a story. It is free, but for $2.99 you can get all the add-ons.

- **Felt Board (www.softwaresmoothie.com):** This app is a virtual felt board that students can use for storytelling. The app costs $2.99.

- **Sock Puppets (http://tinyurl.com/luznt6n):** This free app allows you to create a play with sock puppets, recording your students' voices and automatically syncing them to the puppets. $1.99 gets all the extras.

- **iBook Author (www.apple.com/ibooks-author):** This app is free and is an amazing way for teachers and/or students to create iBooks. There are galleries, videos, interactive diagrams, 3D objects, mathematical expressions, and much more!

WEBSITES FOR STORYTELLING

- **PebbleGo (www.pebblego.com):** This website from the publisher Capstone has taken their books and made them digital. They include print, pictures, video, and audio and are great for researching at the K–3 level. The articles are leveled, and the site is interactive. The cost is steep at $395 to $995/year, depending on what package you choose.

- **Little Bird Tales (www.littlebirdtales.com):** This website is free. Students can draw original artwork and import pictures to create and write stories. To download as an MPG4 is 99 cents. However, printing stories is free.

- **Storyline Online (www.storylineonline.net):** This great website has professional actors and actresses reading quality children's fiction. You get to see all of the pictures, just as if you were listening to a live read-aloud. The site is free.

- **Project Gutenberg (www.gutenberg.org/):** Project Gutenberg offers over 50,000 free ebooks: choose among free epub books, free kindle books, download them or read them online. They carry high quality ebooks. They have been digitized and diligently proofread. No fee or registration is required.

Math Resources

THERE ARE TWO MAIN SETS OF STANDARDS, processes and practices, for the Common Core Math standards. First, you have the math targets, written similarly to ELA (Counting and Cardinality; Operations & Algebraic Thinking; Number

& Operation in Base Ten; Measurement & Data; and Geometry). While you work with students on mathematical processes such as counting and cardinality in first grade, you need to teach them how to apply the Standards for Mathematical Practices, such as problem solving and precision, to those processes. One practice, the only one that includes technology, is mathematical practice 5, "Use appropriate tools strategically."

Following is the explanation CCSS provides for MP5. As this is the standard explanation for grades K–12, it does include references to higher grades.

MP5 | MATH

Use appropriate **tools** strategically.

Mathematically proficient students consider the available tools when solving a mathematical problem. These tools might include pencil and paper, concrete models, a ruler, a protractor, **a calculator, a spreadsheet, a computer algebra system, a statistical package, or dynamic geometry software**. Proficient students are sufficiently familiar with tools appropriate for their grade or course to make sound decisions about when each of these tools might be helpful, recognizing both the insight to be gained and their limitations. For example, mathematically proficient high school students analyze graphs of functions and solutions generated using a graphing calculator. They detect possible errors by strategically using estimation and other mathematical knowledge. When making mathematical models, they know that technology can enable them to visualize the results of varying assumptions, explore consequences, and compare predictions with data. Mathematically proficient students at various grade levels are able to identify relevant external mathematical resources, such as **digital content** located on a website, and use them to pose or solve problems. They are able to use **technological tools** to explore and deepen their understanding of concepts.

Because this description does not give examples for all grades, we have provided a list of appropriate apps, websites, and software and included lessons that will help translate this standard for first grade.

Your students will be using technology as a tool to help them become better at math. That is essentially what this math standard—the only one that explicitly includes technology—states. Using technology as a mathematical practice tool can be interpreted in many different ways. Using technology as a mathematical practice tool can be interpreted in many different ways. In any case, students should use technology tools as often as possible. Fortunately, there are many math programs, websites, and apps available. The best of them have students learning in creative ways and are not just electronic worksheets. They automatically adapt to the students' skill levels and tell you where the students are in their learning and what they need to effectively continue. Of course, these usually do not come free. Following are many good math resources. Some are free and some are not. The free resources (many with ads) are often less interesting to students and not as well organized. They don't give you the feedback you need. However, you must make the decision about what is best for your circumstances and budget.

WEBSITES FOR MATH

- **XtraMath (www.xtramath.org):** This free site is a great resource created by a nonprofit group. It tracks student progress, and students can work on their accounts from home. The main focus is basic math facts.

- **ScootPad (www.scootpad.com):** This is a web-based math site that is totally customizable for individual students. It adapts to the student and keeps the teacher in the loop with multiple reports. It is completely aligned to the CCSS. The price for a class varies from $5 to $20/month.

- **PBS LearningMedia (www.pbslearningmedia.org):** This site is a great source for classroom-ready, free digital resources.

- **Prodigy (www.prodigygame.com):** This is an online adaptive math practice site wrapped in role-playing adventure from Canada. The base price is free with optional paid upgrades with membership.

- **IXL (www.ixl.com/math/):** This online site features adaptive individualized math through gameplay. It gives students immediate feedback and covers many skills, despite its emphasis on drills. Levels range from pre-kindergarten to 8th grade. Class price is $199/year.

- **Sumdog (www.sumdog.com):** This is an online adaptive, straightforward set of math games. Also, there are apps available for tablets and minis. It is free, but you can get more programs, reports, and so on if you purchase an upgrade. However, the upgrade is not necessary to use the site.

- **BrainPOP Jr. (www.brainpop.com):** Top-notch educational videos for elementary school teachers. However, most are Flash and don't work with iPad unless you have an additional Flash player app. Price is $85 to $145.

- **BBC: Schools: Numeracy (http://tinyurl.com/y9k7xj):** This site has many great online interactive math products that are free, without ads, and organized by skill, although you won't be able to track your students' progress.

- **PrimaryGames (http://tinyurl.com/72ojhan), Coolmath-Games (Coolmath-Games. com), SoftSchools (SoftSchools.com),** and **Sheppard Software (http://tinyurl. com/ccrxoa)** are several sites that have free math games that cover all math topics at each grade level. However, these sites have ads, are not able to keep track of a student's success rate, and are not generally self-adaptive to the student's own skill level.

- **Kindersite (www.kindersite.org):** A free site that does not have ads, but you will need to search through the games to find those appropriate to the skill you need. Moreover, it will not keep track of your students' success rate. The games are not adaptive to the student's own skill level.

APPS FOR MATH

- **Explain Everything (www.explaineverything.com):** This $2.99 app uses text, video, pictures, and voice to present whatever your students are asked to create. It is very useful for explaining math concepts and creating visual math.

- **DreamBox Learning Math (www.dreambox.com):** Individualized, adaptive game-based math that keeps kids coming back for more. Available online or through an app. Price is $12.95/month (home) or $25/month (school), less if packaged.

- **Bugs and Bubbles (http://tinyurl.com/hdr3bxe):** Fascinating graphics engage as PK–1 kids practice pre-reading and STEM skills while adapting to their level of skills. Price for app is $2.99.

- **Todo K-2 Math Practice (http://tinyurl.com/pm6tmlk):** One arithmetic app fulfills the needs of many learners in K–2, and the app is free.

- **Teachley: Addimal Adventure (http://tinyurl.com/p2ub7eo):** A well-done app that concentrates on K–2 addition using learning research and strategies through a fun, graphical set of games. Includes the ability to track students' progress and method of learning. Free.

- **Jungle Time (www.jungleeducation.com):** Students learn to tell time in this customizable app. The clocks are easy to read, and there are eight different languages available within the single app. Price is $2.99.

- **Elmo Loves 123s (http://tinyurl.com/na72o4b):** This app is for iPad and Android.

Sesame Street sets the standard for teaching numbers with characters kids love. The app price is $4.99.

- **Mystery Math Town** and **Mystery Math Museum (www.artgigapps.com):** Fun, well-designed customizable app with a clever storyline to pull kids in to solve the mystery while they solve math problems requiring strategy and critical thinking. For grades 1–6. Can have multiple users. Each app is $2.99.

- **Love to Count by Pirate Trio (http://tinyurl.com/jwvvjtp):** Built for PK–2 students, this app has hundreds of tasks and swashbuckling fun for new math learners. The price for the app is $3.99.

- **Motion Math: Hungry Fish (http://tinyurl.com/prms6x5):** Six games build mental math skills and promote fact fluency with a fish hungry for numbers. Price for the app is $1.99.

DIGITAL MATH GAMES

Many studies in recent years have shown how math games can increase student learning. In addition, a survey released in late summer 2014 from the **Games and Learning Publishing Council (http://tinyurl.com/pqms3nj)** indicates that the use of digital games in the classroom is becoming more popular with teachers. According to the survey, 55% of teachers who responded have students play digital games in their classrooms weekly.

With this research and study in mind, the week of the 100th day of school is a perfect time for your students to do some fun activities on the computer that are related to the number 100. First, watch the BrainPOP, Jr. video "One Hundred" on the interactive whiteboard. Then, have students try to identify the mystery word on a hundred chart and a mystery picture by connecting the dots from 1 to 100. Following are some websites that offer fun 100th day of school activities to try at the computer.

- **Splat Square (http://tinyurl.com/38exsd):** This is a hundred grid game, which can be played electronically or printed out. Teacher "calls out" a specific number as the target and students find the number and "splat" it.

- **Mathwire (mathwire.com):** Many standards-based math activities for the 100th day of school!

- **Give the Dog a Bone (http://tinyurl.com/btnmg):** An interactive game where students try to find the 10 hidden bones on the hundreds chart in less than a minute.

- **100 Snowballs (http://tinyurl.com/6jyuvuk):** Another interactive activity that gives students the chance to play and have fun in the snow! Students click and drag snowballs around in the snow, creating any scene they desire—as long as they use only 100 snowballs!

- **TVO Kids (http://tinyurl.com/pnmu89s):** Many 100th day of school interactive math games and perfect for differentiating! Games are in two categories: 2 to 5 years of age; and 11 and under. Many other math and reading games are on this site as well.

Literacy Lessons

Cross-curriculum planning is encouraged with the CCSS by using ELA standards in history, science, and technical subjects. How will you ever get through everything if you teach standard by standard? The key to planning with the CCSS is to teach multiple standards in one lesson. We strongly encourage doing this when possible. We hope the following list of sample lessons for first grade will inspire you to become an effective technology lesson planner.

NARRATIVE WRITING

A first grade teacher recently shared a lesson with us that uses Puppet Pals. The assignment was to write a narrative story. Using Puppet Pals, students created a project to share with the class. When the students shared, they took the time to ask and answer questions about their projects. This simple lesson satisfies **RI.1.5** to teach electronic menus and icons, if you take the time to teach those skills when you introduce Puppet Pals to the class. This lesson's primary focus is satisfying **W.1.6**, which uses digital tools to produce and publish writing collaboratively. Also satisfied is **SL.1.2**, by having students ask and answer questions in text read in other media, as well as **SL.1.5**, by including visual displays. Next, the teacher took a single picture from each of the Puppet Pals projects and assigned a QR code to each project using a reader like **i-nigma Reader (www.i-nigma.com/i-nigmahp.html)** or **QR Code Generator (www.qr-code-generator.com/)**. A picture from the student's work in Puppet Pals hangs in the hall with the QR code. You can scan the QR code and view the Puppet Pal project through an app on a smartphone or other digital devices that have a camera.

RETELL/RECOUNT STORIES

Many teachers in first grade use The Daily 5 during their literacy block. Students choose a book they have practiced reading to themselves or a friend. Using Sock

Puppets, students record their retell or recount of the chosen book. A suggestion might be to help students organize their thoughts by providing a simple storyboard graphic organizer so students can plan their recount or retell scenes before they begin their work on Sock Puppets. The primary focus for this lesson satisfies **W.1.6**, which uses digital tools to produce and publish writing collaboratively. Also satisfied is **SL.1.2**, by asking and answering questions in text read in other media, and **SL.1.5**, by including visual displays.

Social Studies and Science Lessons

The following example lessons address CCSS ELA standards and teach lessons based on national standards in social studies and science.

ANIMALS

This lesson plan idea has students using PebbleGo to research animals and how they survive. Using Wixie, students draw the animal, including habitat, predators, adaptations of body parts that help them survive, and so on. Students narrate their pictures. All pictures are put together into a class zoo ebook. Student books can be saved as a class book on the class ebook shelf. You can be creative and use this for any primary science topic. This lesson satisfies **RI.1.5** to teach electronic menus and icons, especially if you point out to students, when using PebbleGo, how they can navigate the site's menus and icons. This lesson's primary focus satisfies **W.1.6**, which uses digital tools to produce and publish writing collaboratively. Also satisfied is **SL.1.2**, by asking and answering questions in text read in other media, and **SL.1.5**, by including visual displays.

FAMOUS AMERICANS

To enhance a social studies lesson, a teacher shared that she uses Puppet Pals during the month of January and February. Students make a slideshow to explain and illustrate what they know and learned about Martin Luther King, Abraham Lincoln, and George Washington. Student work can be compiled into one slideshow and displayed for parents. Once again, the primary focus for this lesson satisfies **W.1.6**, which uses digital tools to produce and publish writing collaboratively. Also satisfied is **SL.1.2**, by narrating what they learned about the famous men, and **SL.1.5**, by including visual displays. Students can have the characters moving around and even include speech bubbles to bring their characters to life.

Math Lessons

The following two sample lessons address CCSS math standard **MP5**.

GEOMETRY ACTIVITY

To help teach geometry, a teacher used this activity to enhance her lessons on shapes. Each day the classroom has a "shape of the day." Students (working individually or in partners) use iPads or digital cameras to take pictures of that shape, which they look for around the classroom or school. Using a favorite media publishing tool (Wixie, eBook, iBook Author, etc.), students download their pictures. Each shape becomes a chapter in their digital shape book. For each picture taken, students write a sentence or two about their picture. For example, "The hall floor tiles are squares. There are 45 squares from our room to the cafeteria." To differentiate, some students may record all they have learned about squares. For example, "Squares have 4 sides. The sides of squares are all equal. A square is a quadrilateral." Students then share their finished shape books with the class. Books can be checked out and read by other classmates during center time. This activity satisfies **W.1.6**, to produce and publish writing, including collaboration with peers. Furthermore, **SL.1.5** is addressed, as students are adding their digital photos (visual displays) to descriptions of their shapes. This would also cover the **MP.1.5** by using digital tools to enhance mathematical learning.

CLASS ADDITION STRATEGIES

After teaching addition strategies, ask each student to make a page for the class ebook that explains their favorite method for adding. Using your favorite media publishing tool (Wixie, ebook, iBook Author etc.), pair students to write and illustrate their favorite addition strategy. There will be duplicates—and that is OK, as every illustration and explanation is different. Encourage students to make their own drawings to go along with their strategy. They may need your help to locate and download a picture from the internet. Simply search the terms to find pictures for strategies such as Ten Frame or Rekenrek.

Following are some additional strategies for teaching addition.

- Doubles

- Split numbers

- Draw a picture

- Count on fingers

- Counters

- Use a number line

Each page should include a heading for the strategy. As a class, making a table of contents as well as a glossary will help students learn and apply text features to math and thus satisfy **RI.1.5**. Finished books can be shared with the class, placed on a class ebook shelf, or shared with each student in their electronic math folder. Encourage students to frequently refer back to this electronic book to view all the different strategies. Making a similar book with subtraction strategies is a great way to ensure that your students are learning addition and subtraction strategies all year. Students should also be encouraged, as they learn and/or find new strategies, to add them to the electronic addition and subtraction books. This activity satisfies **W.1.6**, to produce and publish writing, including collaboration with peers. Furthermore, **SL.1.5** is addressed, as students are adding their digital photos (visual displays) to descriptions of their addition or subtraction strategies. This would meet **MP.1.5** by using digital tools to enhance math learning. Projecting the book, as well as having a class discussion where students answer questions about the material presented in the strategy book, would satisfy **SL.1.2**.

A Final Note

It is clear that as students progress through the primary grades, they are establishing their baseline of proficiency in technology. This will definitely enhance their experiences with technology in the upper grades, as well as satisfy the CCSS performance standards at the K-2 level. We hope that you found the resources and lesson ideas presented in this chapter useful and that they are easy to adapt to your class.

You will find more resources online at **our website (http://tinyurl.com/oexfhcv)**, which may be helpful to you and could be useful as you look to differentiate your instruction. Visit our online site for updated information about this book. To learn more about meeting technology standards found within the CCSS in other grades, look for our three additional titles in this series.

Chapter 10

Practical Ideas for Second Grade

We realize that you will want to focus on your particular grade or subject when you are planning your lessons and implementing CCSS, so we have organized the Practical Ideas chapters by grade level, then subject. Each grade starts with an overview followed by ELA technology standards with accompanying apps, software, and websites that you can use to help your students have success with that standard. We then continue with the math standard for the grade level, also with accompanying resources. Finally, we have included some sample lessons for each grade level in various subject areas. Although we intend for you to seek your specific grade and subject to help you implement CCSS for your students, please do not disregard other sections of this chapter. To see grades other than K–2, look for our three additional titles in this series, as they could provide information to help you differentiate for students at all levels of your class.

Your second grade students will increasingly be asked to use technology in their learning. One second grade standard that includes technology is exactly the same as its first grade counterpart (**W.2.6**). Other second grade standards have slight to significant variations (**RI.2.5, SL.2.2, SL.2.5**) and two are completely new tech standards for the students coming into second grade (**RL.2.7, L.2.4e**). Although it is not stated in the second grade standards that you should teach typing, by third grade, students will need to be learning to type. In addition, by fourth grade, students will be expected to type one page in a single sitting. As students will be typing more this year, it is important to start teaching them proper typing skills so they do not form bad habits. You don't need to spend too much extra time on this skill. Even the basics would really help when they become third graders. Have an introduction showing students how to use home key positioning, how to use the shift and space key, and discuss proper posture. During writing time, monitor students who are using keyboards as you walk around the room.

Reading Resources

RL.2.7	READING LITERACY

Use information gained from the illustrations and words in a print or **digital text** to demonstrate understanding of its characters, setting, or plot.

YOUR STUDENTS WILL ALREADY HAVE some background in electronic menus and icons from their first grade experiences. Gaining information from digital texts will be a new addition to their previous standard in first grade, though they should have experience using digital tools in the previous year and should have a general understanding of character, plot, and setting. Luckily, there are some great apps, software, and internet sites that are a perfect fit for standard **RL.2.7**. Following are some practical tools for teaching and using digital text in second grade reading.

APPS

- **Toontastic (www.launchpadtoys.com):** Students use visuals to tell stories that they can collaborate on and share with others. The app Toontastic Jr. is free with a few backgrounds. Upgrade for $9.99 or purchase classroom sets discounted depending on the number of students.

- **Explain Everything (www.explaineverything.com):** This $2.99 app uses text, video, pictures, and voice to help students create their own stories with character, setting, and plot.

- **StoryBuddy 2 (www.tapfuze.com/storybuddy2):** This app is easier to use than Explain Everything, but not as versatile. You can use it to create stories with pictures that can be recorded, printed, and read aloud. $3.99

- **Puppet Pals (http://tinyurl.com/qbgaks2):** This app allows students to create a puppet production using familiar characters to create a setting and tell or retell a story. It is free, but for $2.99 you can get all the add-ons.

- **Felt Board (www.softwaresmoothie.com):** This app is a virtual felt board that students can use for storytelling. The app costs $2.99.

- **Sock Puppets (http://tinyurl.com/luznt6n):** This free app allows you to create a play with sock puppets recording your students' voices and automatically syncing them to the puppets. $1.99 gets all the extras.

WEBSITES

- **PebbleGo (www.pebblego.com):** This website from the publisher Capstone has taken their books and made them digital. They include print, pictures, video, and audio, and are great for researching at the K–3 level. The articles are leveled, and the site is interactive. The cost is steep at $395 to $995/year, depending on what package you choose.

- **Little Bird Tales (www.littlebirdtales.com):** This website is free. Students can draw original artwork and import pictures to create and write stories. To download as an MPG4 is 99 cents. However, printing stories is free.

- **Storyline Online (www.storylineonline.net):** This great website has professional actors and actresses reading quality children's fiction. You get to see all of the pictures, just as if you were listening to a live read-aloud. The site is free.

- **Project Gutenberg (www.gutenberg.org):** Project Gutenberg offers over 50,000 free ebooks: choose among free epub books, free kindle books, download them or read them online. They carry high quality ebooks. They have been digitized and diligently proofread. No fee or registration is required.

- **International Children's Digital Library (en.childrenslibrary.org):** This online resource has thousands of digital children's books free. There are many different levels and languages available.

Reading Ideas

RI.2.5	READING INFORMATION

Know and use various text features (e.g., captions, bold print, subheadings, glossaries, indexes, **electronic menus, icons**) to locate key facts or information in a text efficiently.

THERE IS NOT MUCH AVAILABLE for teaching electronic menus and icons, but following are some suggestions. When you are introducing a new piece of software or app to your class, make this standard a part of the lesson. When you look at an internet page, email page, or a word processing document as a class, look at the common menu choices and what options are under each. This standard is primarily to find information in text, so students should also learn how to use search engines and online encyclopedias.

Every time you introduce a new app or piece of software, you should point out the similarities in the menu options, such as where open, print, save, and so on are usually located.

Many icons are standardized in software. Discuss how visual cues help people find information on a page more easily. Discuss the following visual cues and ask students why they think these were chosen, what their meanings are, and make a game of finding them in new programs.

- The printer icon for print

- The magnifying glass for search or zoom in/out

- Arrows for next or forward, last or backward

- Rounded arrows for undo and redo, etc.

- A search box to find information on the page

Tell them how to find and use the spell check feature in different programs, and discuss what cut and paste are in digital terms. Following are some other suggestions for class discussion and exploration.

- Discuss fonts and formatting, such as bolding, underlining, and resizing. Ask why they would use different sizes and formatting for headings and subheadings, etc.

- What are the icons for formatting text? Are they the same in different applications?

- How do these visual cues help them find information on a page more easily?

- Discuss tabs, paragraphs, and how to format a page layout.

- Have students use the "Find" feature to zero in on a certain word or phrase on a digital page.

Writing Resources

> **W.2.6** | WRITING RESOURCES
>
> With guidance and support from adults, use a variety of **digital tools** to produce and publish writing, including in collaboration with peers.

THE SECOND GRADERS IN YOUR CLASS will be coming to you with two years of background in writing using digital resources. To continue this and augment their experiences, you should use as many varied digital tools as possible. Students should now be able to work more independently. They also will be able to collaborate in groups more effectively. Following are some practical tools for using digital tools in second grade writing.

WRITING SOFTWARE

- **Kid Pix (www.kidpix.com):** This software is not free, but it can be used to publish and collaborate on student's writing using pictures and text. There is a new version that features more animation called Kid Pix 3D. For an alternative, try TuxPaint (www.tuxpaint.org). It is a free online download which is also for young students, though somewhat limited.

- **Wixie (www.wixie.com)** and **Pixie (www.tech4learning.com/pixie)**: This software (for purchase) uses multimedia, pictures, sound video, and text to create presentations and stories stored on the cloud for mobile access. The apps are free, but there is an online version for schools with more features that has educational pricing.

- **Kidspiration (http://tinyurl.com/dg2cxa):** A mind-mapping software program that helps student organize their writing. It can be especially helpful for students who are learning to create paragraphs and organize big ideas into their smaller parts. The cost is $40 to $640. Their web-based version is called Webspiration (http://tinyurl.com/bmop3nh) and costs $6/month.

WRITING APPS

- **Popplet (www.popplet.com):** A wonderful online organizational tool for students' writing. A free app called Popplet Lite is also available. It is easy to use and students can import pictures and text to create web maps.

- **Book Creator (www.redjumper.net/bookcreator):** This versatile app can be used to have your students create their own ebooks with pictures, audio, drawing, text, video, and music. Easy for young students to use, but sophisticated enough for high school.

- **Explain Everything (www.explaineverything.com):** This $2.99 app uses text, video, pictures, and voice to present whatever your students are asked to create.

- **StoryBuddy 2 (www.tapfuze.com/storybuddy2):** This app is easier to use than Explain Everything, but not as versatile, so it might be better to use early in the year to create stories with pictures that can be recorded, printed, and read aloud. $3.99

- **Educreations Interactive Whiteboard (www.educreations.com):** This free app is used primarily for teachers to create presentations for their whiteboards, but can be used by students to create expository or narrative writing.

- **Puppet Pals (http://tinyurl.com/qbgaks2):** This app allows students to create a puppet production using familiar characters to tell or retell a story. It is free, but for $2.99, you can get all the add-ons.

- **My Story (www.mystoryapp.org):** A super-easy way to introduce digital book creation to kids. It has good sharing, can be used with multiple authors, and a great interface. This app is $3.99.

- **iBook Author (www.apple.com/ibooks-author):** This app is free and is an amazing way for teachers and/or students to create iBooks. There are galleries, videos, interactive diagrams, 3D objects, mathematical expressions, and much more!

WRITING WEBSITES

- **Fakebook (www.classtools.net/FB/home-page)** and **My Fakewall (http://tinyurl.com/jhrslv6)**: These websites use the popularity of Facebook to encourage writing by creating a Fakebook page or wall posting to write about characters or historical figures. The site is free.

- **Storybird (www.storybird.com):** This free website uses art to inspire storytelling to write, read, share, and print short books.

- **StoryJumper (www.storyjumper.com):** This free site ($24.95 for a hardbound book) gives your students a fun set of tools for writing and illustrating stories that can be shared online.

- **Tikatok (www.tikatok.com):** On this website, there are story starters for Grades

K–6 in ELA, science, and social studies that inspire students to write their own books with artwork to share and print. Classroom price is $19/year. Tikatok StorySpark is the app that you can purchase for $3.

- **Little Bird Tales (www.littlebirdtales.com):** This website is free. Students can draw original artwork, import pictures to create and write stories. To download as an MPG4 is 99 cents. However, you can print stories free.

- **Biblionasium (www.biblionasium.com):** This site makes reading and sharing books fun. It is a virtual bookshelf and review site for students. Teachers can set up free safe accounts for their class. Students rate and review books and keep track of their reading.

- **CAST UDL Book Builder (www.bookbuilder.cast.org):** Use this website to create, share, publish, and read digital books that engage and support diverse learners according to their individual needs, interests, and skills. The site is free.

- **Picture Book Maker (www.culturestreet.org.uk):** This website by culturestreet. org allows students to create six-page stories with background scenes, animals, and props and typing text. Text is limited to roughly two lines per page. Completed stories are displayed with simple page-turning effects. Stories created on Picture Book Maker can be printed. It is a UK funded site, but is currently free internationally.

- **Google Earth (www.google.com/earth):** This free program can be used for many varied purposes even at this age level: mapping students' homes, finding national symbols, and finding places about which they are reading, writing, or sharing.

- **BatchGeo (www.batchgeo.com):** This free (for basic) website works with Google Maps to locate places on a map using coordinates, addresses, and so on. You can upload a series of locations for the site to map and print or paste the map into any digital document.

FREE KEYBOARDING SITES
- **Dance Mat Typing (www.bbc.co.uk/guides/z3c6tfr):** This website by BBC schools teaches typing for younger students.

- **TypingWeb (www.typing.com):** This site has ads, but it does keep track of student progress and allows reports.

Speaking and Listening Resources

SL.2.2	SPEAKING AND LISTENING

Recount or describe key ideas or details from a text read aloud or information presented orally or through **other media**.

SL.2.5	SPEAKING AND LISTENING

Create audio recordings of stories or poems; add drawings or other **visual displays** to stories or recounts of experiences when appropriate to clarify ideas, thoughts, and feelings.

YOUR SECOND GRADE STUDENTS HAVE standards that require them to be able to share through media and create digital pictures or drawings to help them explain something. New to this grade level, along with stories, are poems with which to create audio recordings. Reading poems aloud is a great way to increase fluency with rhythmic pattern and rhyming. The simplest way to help students meet this standard is to have them read to themselves and record their voice using a tape recorder, smart phone, MP3 player, tablet, or computer. **Keynote (www.apple.com/mac/keynote)** is a great program to record voices and keep a yearlong documentation of reading. You can also buy digital books to use with tablets and minis that students can listen to and then recount or draw about the story or poem. There are many apps similar to Keynote in app stores.

Program sites such as **Follett Shelf (http://tinyurl.com/oux56og), TeachingBooks (www.teachingbooks.net),** and **TumbleBooks (tumblebooks.com)** (must be purchased) allow you to have access to multiple ebooks that include fiction as well as nonfiction. You can also check out many ebooks at your local library or purchase them from booksellers such as Amazon or Barnes & Noble (especially if you have e-readers). There are some free ebooks out there. **Storylineonline (www.storylineonline.net)** is a free site, donated by the Screen Actors Guild Foundation, that has some videos of books read by famous people (including *Harry the Dirty Dog* read by Betty White and *Brave Irene* read by Al Gore). Using the websites **Project Gutenberg (www.gutenberg.org), FreeReadFeed (www.freereadfeed.com)** or **Freebook Sifter (www. freebooksifter.com)** is a possibility. There are adult titles on these sites, too, so choose carefully. In general, sites that charge a fee provide a much better selection. Following are some practical technology tools for second grade speaking and listening activities.

FREE WEBSITES WITH DIGITAL BOOKS

- **YouTube (www.youtube.com):** There are many short, free videos that your students can listen to including folktales, science, and people reading popular books that are in your classroom. Your students can listen and then ask and answer questions

- **BrainPOP Jr. (www.brainpop.com):** This is a great resource to use for many areas of your curriculum. There are great video animations and it comes with a questions and answer section. This does cost money, but it is well worth the significant price if you can find the funds. Price is $85 to $145.

- **Wixie (www.wixie.com)** and **Pixie (www.tech4learning.com/pixie):** This software (for purchase) uses multimedia, pictures, sound video, and text to create presentations and stories stored on the cloud for mobile access.

APPS AND WEBSITES FOR STORYTELLING AND PRESENTING IDEAS

- **Toontastic (www.launchpadtoys.com):** Students use visuals to tell stories that they can collaborate on and share with others. The app is free with a few backgrounds. Upgrade for $9.99 or purchase classroom sets discounted depending on the number of students.

- **PebbleGo (www.pebblego.com):** This web site from the publisher Capstone has taken their books and made them digital. They include print, pictures, video, and audio and are great for researching at the K–3 level. The articles are leveled, and the site is interactive. The cost is steep at $395 to $995/year, depending on what package you choose.

- **PowerKnowledge (www.pkearthandspace.com** and **www.pklifescience.com):** This subscription website from Rosen publishers is similar to PebbleGo, but for higher-level readers in grades 3–5. It is useful for second grade students who need a challenge.

- **iMovie (www.apple.com/ios/imovie):** This app ($4.99), which also comes as a program, has many uses in the classroom to create full edited videos or short one-minute trailers. The trailers can be very useful for recounting and presenting ideas to others. There is a free online site to create short videos called Animoto.

- **Explain Everything (www.explaineverything.com):** This $2.99 app uses text, video, pictures, and voice to present whatever your students are asked to create. They can illustrate a story or poem or recount information they hear.

- **Book Creator (www.redjumper.net/bookcreator):** This versatile app can be used to have your students create their own ebooks with pictures, audio, drawing, text, video, and music. Easy for young students to use, but sophisticated enough for high school.

- **StoryBuddy 2 (www.tapfuze.com/storybuddy2):** This app is easier to use than Explain Everything, but not as versatile. You can use it to create stories with pictures that can be recorded, printed, and read aloud. $3.99

- **Puppet Pals (http://tinyurl.com/qbgaks2):** This app allows students to create a puppet production using familiar characters to tell or retell a story. It is free, but for $2.99, you can get all the add-ons.

- **Little Bird Tales (www. littlebirdtales.com):** This website is free. Students can draw original artwork, import pictures to create and write stories. To download as an MPG4 is 99 cents. However, you can print stories free.

- **Felt Board (www.softwaresmoothie.com):** This app is a virtual felt board that students can use for storytelling. The app costs $2.99.

- **ChatterPix Kids (http://tinyurl.com/ptwhtxd):** Take any picture, even of your students, and record their voice to make the pictures lips move with the sound. Great for read aloud and poetry sharing. The app is free.

- **Sock Puppets (http://tinyurl.com/luznt6n):** This free app allows you to create a play with sock puppets, recording your student's voice and automatically syncing it to the puppet. $1.99 gets all the extras.

- **Story Builder (http://tinyurl.com/poxc4rl):** This app is designed to help students improve paragraph formation and integration of ideas and improve higher-level inferencing. Extensive use of audio clips promotes improved auditory processing, and it also has the ability to record narrative. It sells for $7.99.

- **Storyline Online (www.storylineonline.net):** This great website has professional actors and actresses reading quality children's fiction. You get to see all of the pictures, just as if you were listening to a live read-aloud. The site is free.

- **Project Gutenberg (www.gutenberg.org):** Project Gutenberg offers over 50,000 free ebooks: choose among free epub books, free kindle books, download them or read them online. They carry high quality ebooks. They have been digitized and diligently proofread. No fee or registration is required.

- **Starfall (www.starfall.com):** This is a great website with books that students can listen to and/or read. The site is free, but the pay site More.Starfall has a full range of activities with a price of $70 to $270/year.

- **Scene Speak (http://tinyurl.com/qg55sej):** Use it to create visual scene displays and "interactive" social stories. It allows images to be edited and scenes to be linked to create "books" by theme or area of interest. The app is $9.99.

- **Evernote (www.evernote.com):** This is a free app that allows your students to share notes as well as audio and video recordings.

- **Poetry Idea Engine (http://tinyurl.com/2cuowf):** This site from Scholastic allows students to use templates to make different forms of poetry—another great way technology gets kids writing!

SLIDESHOW AND PRESENTATION WEBSITES

- **Prezi (www.prezi.com):** You can sign-up for a free educational account and your students can create and share presentations online. Prezi has mind-mapping, zoom, motion and can import files. Presentations can be downloaded. There is a Prezi viewer app available.

- **RealtimeBoard (www.realtimeboard.com):** This website is an endless white-board, which allows you to enhance your classroom lessons, create school projects, work collaboratively with team members, and so much more. There is a free education version, when you use a school email address. Upgrades are also available.

Language Resources

> ## L.2.4e
>
> Use glossaries and beginning dictionaries, both print and **digital**, to determine or clarify the meaning of words and phrases.

SECOND GRADE IS THE FIRST TIME this standard appears. There is no **L.1.4e**. So using any dictionary will be a new standard for your students. There are fewer child-friendly digital dictionaries and glossaries out there than you might think. These will need introduction and assistance by you. Digital glossaries may be found online through online content. You can also introduce students by using spell check within programs. Many sites, programs, and operating systems have features that allow the user to check the meaning of a word by right clicking or command clicking on it. Following are a few other practical resources that can help second grade students gain understanding.

- **Wordsmyth (www.wordsmyth.net):** This comes with three levels of children's dictionary. When looking up a word, there are also links to a thesaurus and rhyming dictionary for that word. The site is free with ads.

- **Scholastic Storia (http://tinyurl.com/j7awgkd):** This is an ebook reading app that comes with five fiction/nonfiction titles free. There is a built-in glossary to help with difficult words. As of this writing, Scholastic is changing to ebook streaming online at educational prices. See their website for details.

- **TumbleBooks (www.tumblebooks.com):** This website has many wonderful digital stories with accessible glossaries. This online resource does cost. Prices depend on the number of students.

Math Resources

MP5	MATH
Use appropriate **tools** strategically.	

THERE ARE TWO MAIN SETS OF STANDARDS, processes and practices, for the Common Core Math standards. First, you have the math targets, written similarly to ELA (Operations & Algebraic Thinking; Number & Operation in Base Ten; Measurement & Data; and Geometry). While you work with students on mathematical processes operations and algebraic thinking in second grade, you need to teach your students how to apply the Standards for Mathematical Practices, such as problem solving and precision, to those processes. One practice, the only one that includes technology, is mathematical practice 5, "Use appropriate tools strategically."

Following is the explanation CCSS provides for **MP5**. As this is the standard explanation for grades K–12, it does include references to higher grades.

Mathematically proficient students consider the available tools when solving a mathematical problem. These tools might include pencil and paper, concrete models, a ruler, a protractor, **a calculator, a spreadsheet, a computer algebra system, a statistical package, or dynamic geometry software.** Proficient students are sufficiently familiar with tools appropriate for their grade or course to make sound decisions about when each of these tools might be helpful, recognizing both the insight to be gained and their limitations. For example, mathematically proficient high school students analyze graphs of functions and solutions generated using a graphing calculator. They detect possible errors by strategically using estimation and other mathematical knowledge. When making mathematical models, they know that technology can enable them to visualize the results of varying assumptions, explore consequences, and compare predictions with data. Mathematically proficient students at various grade levels are able to identify relevant external mathematical resources, such as **digital content** located on a website, and use them to pose or solve problems. They are able to use **technological tools** to explore and deepen their understanding of concepts.

Because this description does not give examples for all grades, we have provided a list of appropriate apps, websites, and software and included lessons that will help translate this standard for second grade.

Your students will be using technology as a tool to help them become better at math. That is essentially what this math standard—the only one that explicitly includes technology—states. Using technology as a mathematical practice tool can be interpreted in many different ways. Because technology grabs students' attention, supports long-term learning, and makes math fun, students should be encouraged to use math tools as much as possible. There are many math programs, websites, and apps out there. The best of them have students learning in creative ways and are not just electronic worksheets. They automatically adapt to students' skill levels, and they give you the data you need to know where students are in their learning and what they need to advance. We list many good math resources here. Some are free; some are not. The free resources, many with ads, are usually less interesting and not as well organized. They don't give you the feedback you need. It is up to you to decide what is best for your circumstances and budget.

WEBSITES

- **PBS LearningMedia (www.pbslearningmedia.org):** This site is a great source for classroom-ready, free digital resources.

- **XtraMath (www.xtramath.org):** This free site is a great resource that was created by a nonprofit group. It tracks student progress, and students can work on their accounts from home. The focus is basic math facts.

- **ScootPad (www.scootpad.com):** This is a web-based math site that is totally customizable for individual students. It adapts to the student and keeps the teacher in the loop with multiple reports. It is completely aligned to the CCSS. The price for a class varies from $5 to $20/month.

- **Prodigy (www.prodigygame.com):** This is an online adaptive math practice site wrapped in role playing adventure from Canada. The base price is free with optional paid upgrades with membership.

- **IXL (www.ixl.com/math):** This online site features adaptive individualized math through gameplay. This gives students immediate feedback and covers many skills, despite its emphasis on drills. Levels from pre-kindergarten to 8th grade. Class price is $199/year.

- **BrainPOP Jr. (www.brainpop.com):** Top-notch educational videos for elementary school teachers. However, most are Flash and don't work with iPad unless you have an additional Flash player app. Price is $85 to $145.

- **BBC: Schools: Numeracy (http://tinyurl.com/y9k7xj):** This site has many great online interactive math products that are free, without ads, and organized by skill, although you won't be able to track your students' progress.

- **Starfall (Starfall.com):** This free website has a few clever activities for early literacy and math exploration, but the pay site More.Starfall has a full range of activities with a price of $70 to $270/year.

- **Math Blaster HyperBlast (www.mathblaster.com):** The classic game many teachers used when they were students, now updated. Price $0.99 to $1.99.

- **PrimaryGames (http://tinyurl.com/72ojhan), Coolmath-Games (Coolmath-Games. com), SoftSchools (SoftSchools.com),** and **Sheppard Software (http://tinyurl. com/ccrxoa):** are several sites that have free math games that cover all math topics at each grade level. However, they have ads, are not able to keep data on a student's success rate, and are not generally self-adaptive to the student's own skill level.

- **Kindersite (www.kindersite.org):** A free site that does not have ads, but you will need to search through the games to find those appropriate to the skill you need. Moreover, it will not keep track of your students' success rate. The games are not adaptive to the student's own skill level.

- **TenMarks (www.tenmarks.com):** This online site allows students to practice math skills in a supportive and adaptive environment. Based on the new CCSS standards and with plenty of teacher data, differentiation, and support. A single class is free. Site upgrade costs. Math skills through high school level.

APPS

- **Explain Everything (www.explaineverything.com):** This $2.99 app uses text, video, pictures, and voice to present whatever your students are asked to create. Very useful for explaining math concepts and creating visual math.

- **DreamBox Learning Math (DreamBox.com):** Individualized, adaptive game-based math that keeps kids coming back for more. Available online or through an app. Price is $12.95/month (home) or $25/month (school), less if packaged.

- **Todo K-2 Math Practice (http://tinyurl.com/pm6tmlk):** One arithmetic app fulfills the needs of many learners from K–2. In addition, the price is free!

- **Todo Telling Time (http://tinyurl.com/o4qflz5):** Well-done time-telling app that covers time from minutes to months. Price for app is $3.99.

- **Sumdog (www.sumdog.com):** This is an online adaptive, straightforward set of math games. Also, there are apps available for tablets and minis. It is free, but you can get more programs, reports, and so on if you purchase an upgrade. However, the upgrade is not necessary to use the site.

- **Teachley: Addimal Adventure (http://tinyurl.com/p2ub7eo):** A well-done app that concentrates on K–2 addition using learning research and strategies through a fun, graphical set of games. Includes the ability to track students' progress and method of learning. Free app.

- **Love to Count by Pirate Trio (www.nextisgreat.com):** Built for PK–2 students, this app has hundreds of tasks and swashbuckling fun for new math learners. The price for the app is $3.99.

- **Pet Bingo (http://tinyurl.com/nceqqko):** This app is adaptable to each student's level and will have students practicing math facts, measurement, and geometry while enjoying it with their very own pet. There is progress monitoring. Price for the app $1.99.

- **Motion Math: Hungry Fish (http://tinyurl.com/prms6x5):** Six games build mental math skills and promote fact fluency with a fish hungry for numbers. Price for the app is $1.99.

- **Jungle Time (www.jungleeducation.com):** Students learn to tell time in this customizable app. The clocks are easy to read, and there are eight different languages available within the single app. Price is $2.99.

- **Jungle Coin (www.jungleeducation.com):** Students use realistic coins to learn how to count money. There are eight different languages, and U.S. dollars, Euros, and Canadian coins are available within the single app. Price is $2.99.

- **Geoboard (http://tinyurl.com/kzyxjv7):** This app is a digital recreation of a geoboard. The app is simple to use, and the geometry activities are open-ended and endless. The app is free.

- **Swipea Kids Learning Puzzles (www.swipea.com):** This is a digital version of tangrams where students can manipulate, flip, and rotate shapes to create different pictures. App is free. Full upgrade is $0.99.

DIGITAL MATH GAMES

Many studies in recent years have shown how math games can increase student learning. Also, a survey released in late summer 2014 from the Games and Learning Publishing Council (http://tinyurl.com/pqms3nj) indicates that the use of digital games in the classroom is becoming more popular with teachers. According to the survey, 55% of teachers who responded have students play digital games in their classrooms weekly.

With this research in mind, the week of the 100th day of school is a perfect time for your students to do some fun activities on the computer that are related to the number 100. First, watch the BrainPOP, Jr. video "One Hundred" at the interactive whiteboard. Then, try to find out the mystery word on a hundred chart and a mystery picture by connecting the dots from 1 to 100. Here are some fun activities to try at your computer:

- **Splat Square (http://tinyurl.com/38exsd):** This is a hundred grid game, which can be played electronically or printed out. Teacher "calls out" a specific number as the target and students find the number and "splat" it.

- **Mathwire (mathwire.com):** Many standards-based math activities for the 100th day of school!

- **Give the Dog a Bone (http://tinyurl.com/btnmg):** An interactive game where students try to find the 10 hidden bones on the hundreds chart in less than a minute.

- **100 Snowballs (http://tinyurl.com/6jyuvuk):** Another interactive activity that gives students the chance to play and have fun in the snow! Students click and drag snowballs around in the snow, creating any scene they desire—as long as they use only 100 snowballs!

- **TVO Kids (http://tinyurl.com/pnmu89s):** Many 100th day of school interactive math games and perfect for differentiating! Games are in two categories: 2 to 5 years of age; and 11 and under. Many other math and reading games are this site as well.

Literacy Lessons

Cross-curriculum planning is encouraged within the CCSS by the inclusion of ELA standards in history, science, and technical subjects. However, we encourage you to go further and include the arts, math, and physical education in your planning. We also highly encourage teaching more than one standard in a lesson when you can to ensure that you address them all. This is the key to planning with the CCSS. We hope that the following list of a few sample lessons for second grade will inspire you to become an effective technology lesson planner.

FLAT STANLEY

Second grade teachers love to use the book Flat Stanley to teach a variety of literacy and technology standards. After reading the book, students are encouraged to bring or send Flat Stanley some place in the world for an adventure. After each Flat Stanley is returned to the class, students use Google Earth to locate and place mark at least five places the Flat Stanleys from class have traveled. Students choose a few states within the United States and a couple of countries on other continents. Have your students try this activity and then look up the distance Flat Stanley traveled to various places. See if students can find out how long it would take to get there from your school's location. Students can also explore those locations when finished. Using the BatchGeo map, students will be able to see all the locations the Flat Stanleys from your class traveled to this year. This engaging lesson satisfies **RI.2.5**, as students will get to know and use various text features and to locate key facts or information in a text efficiently, specifically with the Google Earth app or program. Students can also recount or retell the story Flat Stanley, including where their Flat Stanley has traveled. This can be illustrated and narrated in a Wixie slideshow. This activity satisfies **RL.2.7**. Wixie slideshows can then be saved to a class ebook shelf, which can be available to other students. This would then satisfy **SL.2.2** and **SL.2.5**.

RETELL/RECOUNT STORIES

Yet another activity second grade teachers have shared with us is having students use Puppet Pals to give a recount or retell of a book. Students take pictures of scenes from the book using tablets. Next, they use the puppets provided in Puppet

Pals or add their own picture (by taking and uploading their picture with a tablet). They can also use a character from the book by taking a picture with a tablet and then uploading and cropping it to fit. Or, students can take a picture of a friend using a tablet. Students next record their recount/retell version. Teachers we have worked with provide a simple graphic organizer for students to use, which helps students outline their thoughts before they begin to record. All recounts/retells are saved, and the class can check out their classmates' recounts and retells. This simple lesson satisfies **RI.2.5**, to teach electronic menus and icons, if you take the time to teach those skills when you introduce Puppet Pals to the class. This lesson's primary focus is satisfying **W.2.6**, which uses digital tools to produce and publish writing collaboratively. Also satisfied is **SL.2.2** by asking and answering questions in text read in other media and **SL.2.5** by including visual displays. Then, using a reader like **i-nigma Reader (www.i-nigma.com/i-nigmahp.html)** or **QR Code Generator (www.qr-code-generator.com)**, teachers can take a single picture from each of the Puppet Pals projects and assign a QR code to each project. A picture from student work in Puppet Pals can then hang in the hall with a QR code, allowing anyone to scan QR codes and view the Puppet Pals projects through any camera-enabled smart device.

Science and Social Studies Lessons

Sample lessons below address CCSS ELA standards and teach lessons based on national standards in social studies and science.

EARTH MOVIE TRAILER

An integrated science activity students can do is research an Earth event using PebbleGo. You will need to give your students a storyboard graphic organizer first, so they can organize their ideas. Using the iMovie Trailer app, students make a movie trailer for their Earth event using pictures they find on the internet or from a book. Students make sure to include titles, subtitles, and keywords to describe their Earth event. Students also select music to fit the event and import it into the iMovie Trailer. This highly motivating activity satisfies many CCSS, including **RL.2.7**, **RI.2.5**, **W.2.6**, and **SL.2.5**.

ECONOMY LESSON

Another option is to teach a social studies lesson on the economy with technology. BrainPOP has several videos on the economy that explore needs, wants, goods, and services. Discuss the definitions, as well as examples of each. Having students take notes in a flipbook or making an anchor chart for the classroom would be beneficial. Using the BrainPOP vocabulary guide, or other online dictionaries, students can clarify the meanings of the vocabulary words: needs, wants, goods, and services. Having students look up words to gain clarity is a nice way to satisfy **L.2.4e** and help students determine or clarify meanings of words. Two of our former colleagues each had a different and unique way to assess this lesson. One teacher had students use Explain Everything to write, draw examples, and record what they learned about goods, services, needs, and wants. **SL.2.2** is satisfied with this project by describing key ideas or details and presenting them through other media. **SL.2.5** is also satisfied by adding visual displays to clarify ideas, thoughts, and feelings.

ECONOMY DEFINITIONS

Teachers we met from another district had students use QR codes to display what they had learned. Students divided their paper into fourths and had the definition (one in each quadrant) of needs, wants, goods, and services. Underneath the definition, students had 3-5 QR codes showing examples of their definition. Students can either take digital pictures or draw pictures, scan, and upload to their tablet before converting to QR codes. This lesson's focus satisfies **W.2.6**, which uses digital tools to produce writing. Also satisfied is **SL.2.2**, by asking and answering questions in text read in other media, and **SL.2.5**, by including visual displays. This is a great project to hang in the hallway for conferences. Parents can just scan the QR code through an app on their smartphone or digital device.

Math Lessons

The following two sample lessons satisfy the **MP5** math standard as well as ELA standards.

MATH ARRAYS

Another activity that a teacher suggested to us is for second grade math. Using Wixie, students take a tablet around school, snapping pictures of any arrays they find. This can easily be done in a 20-minute guided math station rotation. Once back in the classroom, students import their pictures into Wixie and make an arrays slide show. They write the repeated number sentences under each array. All of the students' slides can be saved into a class collection of arrays. This can be a Wixie book so students can read each other's math collections. This activity satisfies **W.2.6**, to produce and publish writing, including collaboration with peers. Furthermore, if students write story problems to go along with their array number sentences, **SL.2.2** and **SL.2.5** will be addressed. This would also cover **MP.2.5** by using digital tools to enhance mathematical learning.

MONEY ACTIVITIES

Second grade teachers we know love this math activity when teaching students about money, specifically making change. This activity can span several days and it can be differentiated easily. Beforehand, identify several sites that sell children's toys. Divide your students into pairs or groups of three. Each team is given a toy site and $500 to "spend" as they go "shopping." Students keep track of what they buy and how much it costs, as well as subtracting it from their $500 so they know how much change is left. The team closest to $0 is the winner. However, the fun doesn't stop there! Teams need to prove how they spent their money. Using your favorite presentation tool (Wixie, Pixie, Kid Pix, etc.) students design their presentation showing how they spent their money. The presentation should include text features they have learned about, such as title pages and headings. This will satisfy **RI.2.5**, knowing and using various text features learned. Students can draw by hand or copy and paste pictures of their purchases from their site. You may need additional adults to help supervise this activity. Presentations are shown to the class by each team. Don't be surprised if you have some students "challenge" results found! Having students collaborate with others, as well as accept guidance and support from adults, will satisfy **W.2.6**. Writing and presenting the account of how students spent their money will address **SL.2.2** and **SL.2.5**, describing key ideas or details and presenting orally using other media. This would also cover the **MP.2.5** by using digital tools to enhance mathematical learning.

A Final Note

It is clear that as students progress through the primary grades, they are establishing their baseline of proficiency in technology. This will definitely enhance their experiences with technology in the upper grades, as well as satisfy the CCSS performance standards at the K-2 level. We hope that you find the resources and lesson ideas presented in this chapter useful and that they are easy to adapt to your class.

You will find more resources online at **our website (http://tinyurl.com/oexfhcv)**, which may be helpful to you and could be useful as you look to differentiate your instruction. In the meantime, please visit our online site for updated information about this book. To learn more about meeting technology standards found within the CCSS in other grades, look for our three additional titles in this series.

References

DeWitt, P. (2013, July 7). *Take a risk . . . Flip your parent communication!* Retrieved from http://blogs.edweek.org/edweek/finding_common_ground/2013/07/take_a_risk_flip_your_parent_communication.html

Edutopia. (2007). *What is successful technology integration?* Retrieved from http://www.edutopia.org/technology-integration-guide-description

Henderson. A., & Mapp, K. (2002). *A new wave of evidence: The impact of school, family, and community connections on student achievement.* Retrieved from http://www.sedl.org/connections/resources/evidence.pdf

LEAD Commission. (2012). *Parents' and teachers' attitudes and opinions on technology in education.* Retrieved from https://app.box.com/s/nfpkody26rx9prhyqvcd

Meeuwse, K. (2013, April 11). *Using iPads to transform teaching and learning.* Retrieved from http://iteachwithipads.net/2013/04/11/using-ipads-to-transform-teaching-and-learning

National Governors Association Center for Best Practices, Council of Chief State School Officers. (2010). *Common Core State Standards.* Washington, DC: Authors.

New York University. (2007) *National Symposium on the Millennial Student.* Retrieved from http://www.nyu.edu/frn/publications/millennial.student/Millennial.index.html

Partnership for 21st Century Skills. (2004). *The partnership for 21st century skills–Framework for 21st century learning.* Retrieved from http://www.p21.org/about-us/p21-framework

Sammons, L. (2009). *Guided math: A framework for mathematics instruction.* Huntington Beach, CA: Shell Education.

Sammons, L. (2011, September 21). *Guided math: A framework for math instruction.* Retrieved from http://www.slideshare.net/ggierhart/guided-math-powerpointbytheauthorofguidedmath

Strategic Learning Programs. (n.d.). Retrieved fro http://www.iste.org/lead/professional-services/strategic-learning-programs

Swanson, K. (2013, October 1). 5 tips for explaining common core to parents. *THE Journal.* Retrieved from https://thejournal.com/articles/2013/10/01/how-to-explain-common-core-to-parents.aspx

Szybinski, D. (2007). From the executive director. *NETWORK: A Journal of Faculty Development,* (4). Retrieved from http://tinyurl.com/pqwr7va

United States Congress. (2010) Section 1015c. Chapter 28: Higher education resources and student assistance. In Title 20–Education (2010 ed.). Retrieved from http://www.gpo.gov/fdsys/pkg/USCODE-2010-title20/html/USCODE-2010-title20-chap28.htm